"If you've been hurt deeply but can't let go of the bitterness that gnaws at your soul, this beautiful book is for you. Drawing from her deep well of faith and personal experience, Lauren Vander Linden guides you with compassion on a transformative journey toward forgiveness. *I Want to Move On* is more than just a book; it's a lifeline for anyone seeking healing and peace."

— **Jennifer Dukes Lee,** author of *Growing Slow, It's All Under Control,* and *Stuff I'd Only Tell God*

"Like many of you, I have been on the receiving end of pain brought on by others and wrestled with bitterness and unforgiveness to find healing. This book is a thorough exploration of such a journey and how God desires to heal every wound you hold. A beneficial read for the person struggling to find freedom and wanting to finally move on!"

— **Brittany Rust,** pastor, Bible teacher, author

"As Christians, we talk a lot about forgiveness. We expect to be able to forgive and move on. But actually living what we believe is no easy task. We carry hurt, bitterness, and pain for years, even a lifetime. Lauren offers a catalog of human emotions, excuses, and the help we all need to actually move forward and find the freedom Christ offers. Her engaging format and conversational style will meet you wherever you're feeling stuck."

— **Chase Replogle,** pastor and author of *The 5 Masculine Instincts*

"This book was like sitting down and chatting with a friend. Lauren is real and relatable and teaches you how to truly forgive those who have hurt you and the freedom that comes from that. It's backed up with tons of scripture and will help you on the journey of truly healing the pain and bitterness and finding the freedom God desires for you."

— **Brenna Newman,** Bookstagrammer, @brennas_book_corner

"This book is not only full of relatable situations but loaded with practical application to walk through them. Lauren has a way of unpacking the hard emotions we face and providing ways to not only honor others but honor God in the process. I cannot recommend this book enough!"

— **Jessica Doyle,** author of *Growing in Hard Places*

"*I Want to Move On* is the book I wish I had years ago. Forgiveness, redemption, and healing are hard topics, but Lauren brings so much life, clarity, and love to them. With honest vulnerability and rich exposition of God's Word, *I Want to Move On* will give you practical tools to move forward in faith and hope from what has been holding you back."

—**Tara Sun,** author of *Surrender Your Story,* and host of the
Truth Talks with Tara podcast

"Lauren does an incredible job pointing out the proactive tools for forgiveness we all desperately long for. She reminds us of the anchors that are holding us back and to be mindful of how our heart is postured in the hurt. This book will help you refine your focus to find true contentment in what God is doing in your life."

—**Jenni Scherff,** mom and adoption advocate

"This book is both a balm and the best kick in the pants. It is for the weary heart, the wounded spirit, and the one looking for a better way to live in freedom. Lauren Vander Linden has battle-tested the truths in *I Want to Move On.* She is relatable, wise, and exactly the kind of friend you want to help you root out the poison of bitterness and grow something beautiful in its place."

—**Kimberly Stuart,** author of *Star for Jesus (And Other Jobs I Quit)*

"We have all been hurt by someone. It's how we respond that matters. Using real-life experiences, Lauren gives a practical road map to help us move on in a biblical way."

—**Jonathan Palmer,** pastor at Summitcreek Church

"This book hit me at my core. Wronged? Accused? Misunderstood? Lauren writes about it all with honest conversations, gentle truths, and relatable insights from a biblical worldview. Growing through every page, I was realigned and reminded of the powerful freedom that comes when we don't ignore what needs to be addressed *in us.* As you honestly and intentionally navigate through *I Want to Move On,* the strongholds of bitterness and pain will be released!"

—**Casey Gibbons,** lead pastor, author of *A Girl's Life with God,*
founder of Mothergood.us

I WANT TO MOVE ON

BREAK FREE

FROM BITTERNESS

I WANT

AND DISCOVER

TO MOVE

ON

FREEDOM, IN

FORGIVENESS

Lauren Vander Linden

LEAFWOOD
PUBLISHERS
an imprint of Abilene Christian University Press

I WANT TO MOVE ON

Break Free from Bitterness and Discover Freedom in Forgiveness

LEAFWOOD

P U B L I S H E R S

an imprint of Abilene Christian University Press

Copyright © 2024 by Lauren Vander Linden

ISBN 978-1-68426-004-1 | LCCN 2023020336

Printed in the United States of America

LIBRARY OF CONGRESS CATALOGING-IN-PUBLICATION DATA
Names: Vander Linden, Lauren, author.
Title: I want to move on / Lauren Vander Linden.
Description: Abilene : Leafwood Publishers, 2024.
Identifiers: LCCN 2023020336 | ISBN 9781684260041 (paperback) | ISBN9781684268603 (ebook)
Subjects: LCSH: Forgiveness—Religious aspects—Christianity. | Betrayal—Religious aspects—Christianity. | Christian life.
Classification: LCC BV4647.F55 V37 2024 | DDC 234/.5--dc23/eng/20240108
LC record available at https://lccn.loc.gov/2023020336

Cover design by Greg Jackson, Thinkpen Design
Interior text design by Sandy Armstrong, Strong Design

Leafwood Publishers is an imprint of Abilene Christian University Press.
ACU Box 29138 | Abilene, Texas 79699

1-877-816-4455 | www.leafwoodpublishers.com

24 25 26 27 28 29 30 // 7 6 5 4 3 2 1

To my husband, Travis, who supported this dream every step of the way, despite many nights of me shut in my office with no thought given to making dinner. To my parents, Jim and Linda, for teaching me wisdom in navigating difficult situations. To my sister, Elizabeth, for lending an ear during all my challenging seasons. Lastly, to the Holy Spirit, who was my guide, my counselor, and my comforter as I navigated tough situations. I pray everyone reading this book can experience nearness with the Holy Spirit as you work through past hurt.

Contents

ONE

"They HURT Me"

Let's get real. If you picked up this book, chances are the title alone brought back memories. Memories of when someone hurt you to your core. Perhaps they took something from you. And by "took something from you," I don't mean something small. Maybe it was

your reputation,

your dignity,

your marriage,

your friendship,

your job,

or your ideal life.

Perhaps the person who hurt you was close to you, like a significant other, spouse, or best friend. It could be that they were someone you looked up to or held to a high standard, like a pastor, parent, or mentor. Maybe this person was a stranger or part of a group that you feel wronged you or that you hold responsible for something. No matter who it was, something was done to you that stung. It hurt like walking on a thousand needles, and not for the sake of acupuncture.

When I was a kid, my friend and I were at our church campgrounds one time with our moms. As we waited for them, we came up with a game. We kept jumping over ropes that linked wooden posts together. Even though I was only eight years old, none of the posts were particularly tall, but on the last jump, my friend dared me to jump over the highest post.

Easy for her to say. She turned out to be 5'10".

But I was never one to turn down a challenge. I got a running start, jumped, and flipped over the rope. When I stood up, I couldn't breathe. I couldn't speak. I stumbled over to our moms and just stared, trying to make words come out.

Will this be how I die? What just happened?

Our moms were concerned at first until they concluded that I "got the wind knocked out of me." Ease came over them once they recognized that's what it was and that I would be okay.

But I spent about another thirty seconds not being okay.

I was thinking, *What does getting the wind knocked out of you mean? What if it's more serious than that? What if it's too late by the time they realize it?*

They kept saying, "Lauren, you're going to be okay." But I just kept thinking, *When can I breathe next?*

Some of you have been hurt like that, as if someone punched you in the gut and then you couldn't breathe. Like you got the wind knocked out of you. You're not sure if you're going to be okay. You're just trying to breathe.

I remember experiencing my figurative "gut punch" one night while at a mentor's house after receiving a text of a screenshot that sent me over the edge. The screenshot conveyed a group was questioning my integrity around a very private matter and intended to use whatever they could find against me. Upon seeing this, I started crying and shaking as the feelings of being attacked and violated came over me. This had been going on for years, and this was the last straw. Furthermore, in the past these individuals had said they were doing this out of concern for me; although, this was clearly no longer the case. There was a part of me that thought I'd never get over it, and honestly, I didn't want to.

As I tried to calm down, my mind jumped to what my next step should be as a good Christian girl. As someone who grew up in church, it was hard for me to experience any kind of rage without an immediate thought that the right thing to do is to forgive quickly. This made things complicated since I was torn between recognizing my pain and feeling shame for having anger in the first place. My mind knew I needed to forgive the people who I felt were out to get me, but my heart wasn't ready. My emotions were raging.

Instead, I wanted to call them up and yell my entire stream of consciousness. Better yet, I wanted to post what had happened on social media for the world to see.

There. Then I would have justice.

But deep down, I knew that would yield temporary satisfaction that I was likely to regret later. Experience had taught me that doing those types of things would only hurt me more and wouldn't come with the feeling of justice I was so desperately seeking.

But how would I get justice? I couldn't just sit there with those feelings.

But I did just that.

I sat there with those feelings.

Thanks to God's Word, I was wise enough to know that engaging with the people who hurt me in the name of getting justice or, let's be honest, revenge, would have consequences.

I just wasn't wise enough to realize that me sitting with my feelings would have consequences, too.

Remember when I shared that I wasn't ready to forgive even though I knew I should? Hanging on to unforgiveness only produces one thing: bitterness.

I remember watching the Tyler Perry movie *Diary of a Mad Black Woman* when I was younger.

The main character, Helen, had witnessed her husband cheat on her and found out he even fathered children with his mistress.

When another character called Helen "bitter," she responded sarcastically with, "I'm not bitter. I'm mad as heck*!"[1] That quote kept echoing in my mind whenever I thought about my circumstance.

"I'm not bitter! I'm mad as heck!"

Have you ever been there?

You convince yourself that you're anything but bitter. You hear a sermon on bitterness or unforgiveness, and your first thought is, *That's not for me.*

My thought pattern was:

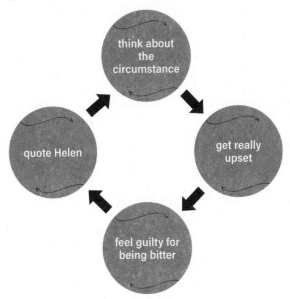

You're simultaneously thinking about the situation that led to bitterness and denying that you need a sermon on it. I think we've all listened to someone speak on unforgiveness only to deny our own feelings for fear of "going back there."

"Denial ain't just a river in Egypt," Mark Twain is famously credited as saying.

Psychologists will tell you that denial is your first response when you recall a stressful or tense situation. The body does this on your behalf as a way to subconsciously prevent those feelings from overwhelming you.[2]

It's nice of your body to try to protect you, but it doesn't allow you to get to the heart of the issue.

Psychologists agree that denial is a short-term solution to long-term pain. Denial doesn't have the power to heal. It doesn't have the power to resolve issues. It only has the power to avoid them.[3]

Denial might look like this:

> *I'm over it. That was a long time ago.*
>
> *It wasn't that big of a deal.*
>
> *I don't need help.*
>
> Or, my most-used one: *I'm fine.*

Have you ever said something similar? I know I have.

There were even times when I would say spiritual-sounding things like, *I'm just leaving it in the Lord's hands.* And while I would encourage us all to do that, I wasn't allowing myself to fully feel the emotion I needed to.

Of course, we can trust every situation with the Lord! But even taking the right steps in the wrong order can keep us from moving forward. We must start by acknowledging our hurt.

If we can't recognize our hurt, we can't heal from it.

That's why accepting the fact that you were hurt is a crucial first step. It kicks denial to the curb and allows you to begin the healing process.

To recognize our hurt, it's important to name the offense. Too often, we excuse, minimize, or shy away from calling out what hurt us. This may be an attempt to offer grace, ignore our feelings, or not stir up drama.

Whatever your reasons, if you can't recognize why you're hurt, forgiveness will be harder. It's hard to forgive someone when you've never articulated why you're upset. It would be no different than a doctor prescribing medicine when you never said what hurt. How could they possibly get to the root of the issue?

The Bible tells us in 2 Corinthians 10:5, "We destroy arguments and every lofty opinion raised against the knowledge of God, and take every thought captive" (ESV). When you read that, it's easy to think that the arguments will only be external. Some of the arguments will be internal, and that doesn't change the fact that we need to take them captive.

I'm asking that of you.

If we're going to make progress, we must take every thought captive and be brutally honest with ourselves. That's where it starts.

There's no hiding our unforgiveness for the sake of looking good. If you're like me, you've probably already tried that. Loopholes to forgiveness don't help you move on.

As we go through this book together, I want us to make some commitments to each other:

- If we sense a feeling of bitterness or hatred toward anything or anyone, we're not going to fight it, deny it, or push it aside. We're going to acknowledge it.
- We're going to name the offense and determine why we feel this way.
- We're going to actively work on releasing it in the moment.

Does that mean even when you just open social media to look something up and see the girl who didn't invite you to her Friendsgiving? Yes.

Does that mean when you're driving down the street and you pass the church whose pastor offended you? Uh-huh.

Does that mean . . . ? Yes. That's the commitment I'm asking us to make to one another.

We cannot actively move on if we do not first admit to ourselves how we're feeling!

As I unpacked my feelings, for some reason, I felt like being mad was better than being bitter. But when we stay mad long enough, we'll find it's all the same thing. Anger, hatred, and bitterness are all cousins. We can compartmentalize them in our minds to justify our anger or validate our hate, but, if left unaddressed, they impact us all the same.

What does it look like when there's bitterness in your life?

Here are some clues:

- You have a hard time making eye contact with "them."
- When someone brings up their name, your heart starts beating faster, and not because you have butterflies.
- At a moment's notice, someone may say something that sends you into a spiral (whether they know it or not).
- You feel as though you are trying to defend yourself and offend them—as if you're playing both defense and offense.
- You have a hard time getting on social media for fear of seeing their content.
- You may have started to become a homebody out of fear of running into them.
- You don't want your friends to be friends with them or to even like them.
- Their success is to your demise, and their downfall pleases you.
- You play circumstances over and over in your mind.

- Someone walks in the room only to find you having a full-fledged fake conversation when you're all by yourself. You win all of those fake arguments because you've had hours, days, or even years to think of the perfect retort that you wish you had thought of in the moment.

Did any of those circumstances resonate with you? I hope so, because that would mean I'm not alone.

I've experienced all of them.

Yes, even the one where someone catches me having a fake conversation—especially the one where someone catches me having a fake conversation.

Remember when I said this is going to be painful? It's not easy for me to share these feelings, because to share that I've experienced them exposes the bitterness I allowed to set in. Some of those feelings may be our gut reaction because we're hurt, but more often than not, they are the result of not dealing with the hurt, and we become bitter.

And bitterness looks ugly on us.

> Bitterness will turn you into someone you're not.
>
> Bitterness will take hold of your heart and make you doubt who you even are.
>
> Bitterness will take you captive. It will make you a slave to your thoughts, to your emotions, and to the person whom you are bitter toward.
>
> Bitterness causes deep pain. It causes a pain deeper than the initial hurt you first experienced.

Because of this, it's more important to expose bitterness and work to get rid of it than to try to pretend like we don't struggle with it.

This is serious stuff.

Satan may try to make us feel like we don't really need to work on our bitterness or emotions because *it's not that bad* or *it happened a long time ago.* But, as we'll see, removing bitterness from our lives will help us walk in fullness and freedom.

For me, forgiveness wasn't found by using "the simple five steps to forgive forever." I kept finding loopholes and reasons to hold on.

My circumstance is different, so I can still act this way, I told myself.

I bet if people knew what they did to me, they'd understand why I'm acting the way I am.

But here's the thing: finding loopholes for forgiveness doesn't help you move on. I finally found healing when I addressed all of the thoughts I had made habitual. Most of them were thoughts that were holding me back from the true freedom forgiveness brings.

Chances are, you've thought these, too.

Each thought that follows is a thought that echoed in my mind on repeat until I made peace with each one. The person who hurt you has a reign over your thought life, and it's time it came to an end. I'll also share the revelations I had with each thought that helped me find freedom. My prayer is that these resonate with you. I am convinced that your best life is on the other side of your bitterness.

You're who I'm writing this book for. And you will heal from the hurt, beat bitterness, and move forward to all God is calling you to!

APPLICATION

What has my thought cycle looked like when dealing with my scenario?

What is my motivation for moving on from these feelings?

Prayer: *Lord, please prepare my heart during these chapters to forgive once and for all. Open my eyes to all you have for me, and show me how holding on to bitterness is negatively impacting me so I may release it for good.*

NOTES

[1] (*except she didn't say heck) *Diary of a Mad Black Woman*, directed by Darren Grant (Santa Monica, CA: Lionsgate Films, 2005).

[2] "Denial: Overview, Effects, and Alternatives," BetterHelp, December 8, 2022, updated September 18, 2023, https://www.betterhelp.com/advice/general/what-is-denial-psychology-how-to-address-it/.

[3] "Denial," BetterHelp.

TWO

"I Know I SHOULDN'T Feel This Way"

was sitting in my first counseling session, and I had just finished pouring my heart out. All my emotions came out, even the ones I had successfully suppressed.

"I know I shouldn't feel this way," I told the counselor sitting across from me. "I'm sorry."

"Why is that?" she probed kindly.

"Because Christians shouldn't feel this way. They should just forgive and move on," I answered.

"Lauren, *do* you feel that way?"

"Yes."

"What you need to understand is that 'should' is not a real word."

"Huh? 'Should' is not a real word?"

She went on to explain that just because you "should" feel a certain way doesn't mean that you do. Whether you "should" or not doesn't change what you are feeling. The word *should* does not depict reality.

As long as we go about our lives trying to force ourselves to feel a certain way because we "should," we won't see real change.

This is hard for me to admit, but:

I felt betrayed by the person who hurt me.

I felt upset with my friends for being friends with the person who hurt me.

I felt hurt that God would continue to use, speak to, or even love the person who hurt me.

I knew I "shouldn't" feel this way, so I tried not to. I tried hard, but it didn't change anything.

I finally understood what my counselor was saying. If I was going to move on, I had to start by giving myself permission to feel the way I did. Even if I was overreacting, was being dramatic, or should just get over it, none of those explanations spoke to the pain I felt.

A Safe Space

Although the feeling of shame is related to denial, it is different. Denial is your body's defense mechanism to protect itself. Denial is suggesting that you don't feel a certain way when you do. Telling yourself that you shouldn't feel a certain way involves shame.

We know we shouldn't be bitter, so we hate ourselves for being bitter.

We know we should forgive, so we pretend like forgiveness is a one-time thing and resent ourselves when feelings come back around. If our emotions strike up again, we feel ashamed that we "failed" at forgiveness.

Whether by way of denial or shame, the worst thing we can do is try to hide our emotions from ourselves and from God.

Maybe while growing up, we gained the false perception that we couldn't be real with God. We came to believe that he loved us a lot but not enough to deal with our true selves. We assumed that he only loved us enough to handle our church selves.

Maybe you've even had the thought, *God loves me when I'm living at peace with others, and he's mad at me when I'm not.*

After my initial hurt, part of Romans 12:18 kept echoing in my head: "As far as it depends on you, live at peace with everyone" (NIV).

But instead of reading this as encouragement, I was ashamed that I was not at peace with people in the body of Christ. This only heightened my need to push my feelings aside so I didn't feel shame.

That's why the first step is to admit to yourself how you feel. The second step is that you need to know it's okay to tell God!

I think about Psalms 13:1–2 (NIV), where David wrote:

> How long, LORD? Will you forget me forever?
> How long will you hide your face from me?
> How long must I wrestle with my thoughts
> and day after day have sorrow in my heart?
> How long will my enemy triumph over me?

Some of this lamenting was about his circumstances, and some of it was lamenting to God about God. That's bold.

Yet, we know God heard this and did not turn away but instead comforted David. He was not afraid of David's feelings, nor did he hold them against David.

That's why for us to release the shame of our feelings, we need to model David and recognize that God is our safe space. God will be more disappointed with your inauthenticity than with your raw feelings.

God is not someone we have to present to. That's a lie to keep you from drawing near to him.

When I think about what our appropriate relationship with God looks like, it involves fear, respect, love, and devotion, but also laughing, crying, pain, and questioning.

The Bible tells us we were made in God's image. Do you really think the tough emotions surprise him? God can handle your questions. He wants to help you carry your pain. His primary goal is your healing and freedom, and that's the reason why he cautions us about allowing bitterness in our hearts.

He knows it's making you miserable, and that's why he's called us to move forward. But his desire for us to heal and move forward doesn't change his recognition that we need someone to talk to, someone to be real with. And he doesn't just prefer that "someone" to be him. He hopes it will be.

He made you who you are. Your feelings are not a surprise to him and do not disqualify you from him.

The next time you feel like you can't share it with God because you "shouldn't feel this way in the first place," remember that God is your safe space.

Maybe you need to skip to the reflection portion of this chapter, take two deep breaths, and let God know how you feel. It's okay. There's more revelation waiting when you come back.

An Easy Yolk?

Have you ever heard anyone refer to Jesus's yoke being easy?

They're referring to Matthew 11:28–30 (NIV), where Jesus promises us this:

> Come to me, all you who are weary and burdened, and I will give you rest. Take my yoke upon you and learn from me, for I am gentle and humble in heart, and you will find rest for your souls. For my yoke is easy and my burden is light.

This passage is powerfully comforting, but the first time I heard it audibly preached in church, I thought it was referring to an egg yolk. I remember thinking, *I believe this, Lord. I just have no clue how the egg yolk ties in.*

A yoke is a wooden frame, commonly used in Jesus's time, that joins two animals together to carry a heavy load. This was typically done with oxen. The yoke would allow for a heavy load to be shared across the two oxen, and together, they would be able to carry a heavier item or load than if they were carrying it on their own.

My husband and I just moved into our first house, and we've had a lot of fun decorating and putting things together. This has led to many purchases of lightly used items at garage sales or online.

I'm excited about each thing my husband brings home until the reality of us unloading and moving it into the house hits me. I can't carry large items like a foosball table, large cabinets, and a refrigerator on my own! Thankfully, I have my husband to share and distribute (most of) the weight to.

In the spirit of transparency, I feel the need to share that I did not even attempt to help move the fridge. We had friends do that.

And just like our friends came to carry a load I could not, that's what God wants to do for you. You can be honest with God because he already knows your emotions. He's inviting you to come to him and is asking to carry your load.

The frustration you feel toward someone? He'll help you with that.

The bitterness in your heart toward the person who wronged you? He wants to see it, know it, and help you through it.

And, just like when I lift things with someone stronger than me, he'll let you take on less of the load.

Let's a take a minute right now and write down some of the feelings we have. Here's a list to get you started (circle the ones you feel, and write to God in the space below):

Betrayal   Hurt   Pain   Confusion

Misdirection   Shame   Guilt   Frustration

Anger   Mistreated   Wronged   Violated

Unloved   Unworthy   Less Than

Additional feelings:

As you look at the feelings circled, I want to reassure you:

You are not bad for feeling this way.

If you're like me when I read books, you may not have circled any, or you may have withheld from circling some that you know you need to because you are ashamed of them. Or maybe you're worried someone else might read it. I'll say it again: you are not wrong for feeling this way.

These are your feelings to fully feel. And God understands.

He understands these feelings so deeply; he knows the impact they will have on your heart. That's why he knows how important it is for you to move forward.

How do we move forward? How do we get rid of these feelings?

The answer is simple: forgiveness.

If you want to move on from the feelings you circled above— feelings like anger, frustration, violation, and bitterness—then forgiveness is your answer.

You probably already knew that. It's probably knowing that you should forgive that's led you to be ashamed of your feelings.

This likely isn't the first time someone has told you forgiveness is the answer, but not everyone knows what it looks like, what steps to take to go through it, and how to forgive.

First, let's admit it to ourselves and let's get real with God: we're tired of feeling this way. And it's time to forgive.

Let's continue to work through our thoughts and counter-truths to find freedom together. The below application is a great place to start.

APPLICATION

What feelings do I need to share with God?

Where have I been holding back?

What are some practical ways I can spend more time with God for him to become my "safe space?"

Scripture: "Pour out your hearts to him, for God is our refuge" (Ps. 62:8 NIV).

Prayer: Rather than give you words to pray, for this chapter, my hope is that you can simply talk to God and share with him what's on your mind as a practical action step to making God your safe space.

THREE

"My BITTERNESS Isn't as Bad as What They Did to Me"

When is bitterness okay? Is there a scale? How much of it can we tolerate?

I knew bitterness was wrong. Like we talked about in the last chapter, I knew I "shouldn't." But "should" does not dictate reality. I started seeking. Is all bitterness wrong? Is it even wrong when it feels justified? Is it wrong if the person is a Christian? Not a Christian? Does it matter if they threw the first punch?

I looked for all the wisdom I could find. To be honest, I was looking for a loophole. After all, the Bible tells us that God gets angry. Even scriptures reference God getting jealous in the Bible.

I'm just being like God, I lied to myself.

But, justified as it may seem, holding on to it didn't help me move on.

We know that God's Word is the ultimate authority, so I turned to the Bible for my answers. And answers I found.

You may be wondering how I found answers in a book that has so many pages. Thankfully, looking for answers in the Bible can be as complicated or as simple as you make it. I just used the word finder in the back of my Bible and looked up everywhere "bitterness" is mentioned.

The first reference I found was in Deuteronomy 29, and it hit me like a ton of bricks. The primary thing I concluded after reading the passage was: *bitterness brings curses instead of blessings.*

Curses? That doesn't seem fair. The person who did me wrong is the one who this should be for! Not me.

While that aligned with my earthly wisdom, Deuteronomy 29 depicts the covenant that the Lord renewed with the Israelites after they came out of Egypt. It's referred to as the covenant of Moab. This covenant was given to the Israelites right before they entered the promised land, and it was God renewing a covenant he had already given to them.

In this covenant, God described who his people were and gave them instructions for how to live. He told them to avoid idolatry so they would be blessed rather than cursed. Specifically, Deuteronomy 29:18–19 (ESV) says:

> Beware lest there be among you a root bearing poisonous and bitter fruit, one who, when he hears the words of this sworn covenant, blesses himself in his heart, saying, "I shall be safe, though I walk in the stubbornness of my heart."

Idolatry, the practice of trusting and following other gods, was the main source of their bitterness. It created a stubbornness and hardness of heart that hurt everyone. Here we see Moses call out a well-known principle that bitter plants can ruin everything in the garden. Therefore, bitterness is not to be tolerated.

Deuteronomy 29:20 tells us that for the person who remains bitter, "The LORD will not be willing to forgive him, but rather the anger of the LORD and his jealousy will smoke against that man, and the curses written in this book will settle upon him, and the LORD will blot out his name from under heaven" (ESV).

If you thought that was bad, you should see what some of the curses detailed in Deuteronomy say! We know that, through Jesus, we are freed from every curse of sin. However, that does not mean there aren't consequences to our actions. Reading the curses in store for the person harboring bitterness made me recognize the unrealized consequences of bitterness and made me even more grateful God had spared me from it.

After unsuccessfully trying to find a version that was less harsh than what I first read, I had no choice but to conclude one thing: bitterness is serious business.

Why? Let's take a look.

Bitterness Produces Bad Fruit

Let's continue to unpack the verses in Deuteronomy since, if you're like me, reading the Old Testament can sometimes feel like reading a different language.

> Beware lest there be among you a root bearing poisonous and bitter fruit. (Deut. 29:18 ESV)

What does the Bible mean by "a root bearing poisonous and bitter fruit"?

Whatever root grows out of the soil is what we name the plant. Think about ginger root—you just call it ginger, but you're actually eating the root. The same goes for other root vegetables like potatoes, carrots, and beets.

In this case, you have a root-bearing bitter fruit, or a bitter plant with a bitter root. Bitterness.

There's another part of the Bible that refers to the fruit that God's people produce.

In the Sermon on the Mount, Jesus warned of false prophets who look like they're followers of Christ but really are enemies of the gospel. Jesus said that just by following this warning, "You can identify them by their fruit, that is, by the way they act" (Matt. 7:16 NLT).

When I think of fruit, I think of summertime. My favorite fruit in the summer is watermelon. I spend a good amount of time picking out my watermelon. It's got to be the right size, the right shape, and the right weight. Watermelons aren't available year-round, and they cost more than most fruit, so I take this decision very seriously.

When you think you've picked out the perfect watermelon and you cut into it only to find it's watery and not sweet, it's upsetting! You must make the decision: *Do I take this watermelon to the party and leave everyone disappointed, or do I go back to the store and try again?*

The same is true when we display bitter fruit. But instead of losing out on seven dollars and the fruit platter you were going to serve, you miss out on something more costly—relationships.

This means that when we have this bitter fruit in our lives, we are not representing the gospel of Christ, we are not acting Christlike, and our fruit suggests we're actually enemies of the gospel.

How many of us have pointed a finger at a person who hurt us and thought, *They're not acting Christlike?*

Our bitter fruit aligns us with the very ones Jesus calls wolves in sheep's clothing (Matt. 7:15).

When I discovered that my bitterness put me in the same boat as my enemy, I was never more determined to jump ship!

If the Bible says to know Christians by our fruit, and if our fruit looks and tastes like everyone else's, why would anyone be attracted to the gospel?

Why would anyone want to join the club? Our fruit tastes bad. No one is signing up for the "bitter fruit of the month" club.

Deuteronomy is referring to a root that produces bitter fruit, much like the roots of bitterness in our hearts.

It's our job to produce fruit that aligns with the Word of God and is sweet like the perfect watermelon on a summer day.

Bitterness Is a Poisonous Root

There's another place in the Bible where we see similar language that references bitterness.

> Look after each other so that none of you fails to receive
> the grace of God. Watch out that no poisonous root of
> bitterness grows up to trouble you, corrupting many.
> (Heb. 12:15 NLT)

Imagine that your heart is fertile soil.

You have plants that take root in your heart—plants like compassion, love, joy, contentment, peace, and other fruits of the Spirit.

When you spend time with God, you are watering those roots in your heart.

But there are also plants that take root that you don't want in your heart. As you think about them and hold on to them, you are watering them, and they continue to grow deeper.

Bitterness is like a root that grows, deepens, and affects the soil around it. That's why the goal of this book isn't just to move on from one situation—it's to continuously live in freedom from any sort of "root" of bitterness.

When I started writing this book, all the different "roots" I allowed in my heart that shouldn't be there became clear.

- The obvious roots of bitterness stemming from unfor-giveness to people that had wronged me
- The root of bitterness that came from comparing myself to certain people
- The root of bitterness I had toward people who think dif-ferently than me
- The root of offense I felt toward random people based on events that happened a long time ago that I never addressed or got over

I had so many roots in my heart that I thought, *Maybe I can keep plants alive for a change!* But as much as I wanted a win for my gardening skills, those roots needed to go.

But the Bible doesn't just say bitterness is a root. Do you notice how this is the second time a root of bitterness is referred to in the Bible and the word *poisonous* has accompanied it?

Harboring bitterness is like drinking poison, but not all at once. It's like taking little sips of poison at every meal.

Some of our to-do lists look like this: get out of bed, make breakfast, take vitamins, drink a teaspoon of poison.

Usually, we're not drinking it in large doses. Rather, it's a slow, consistent poisoning throughout the day by way of our thoughts.

Have you seen the movie *The Princess Bride*? There's a scene where the main character, Westley, faces off with a man who thinks he can outsmart him. Westley comes up with a plan to outwit him. He proposes that he puts poison in one of the glasses, and his enemy will get to decide which glass he'll drink and which glass Westley will drink.

If his enemy can outsmart him and drink the glass without poison, he'll win and Westley will die. Played out the other way, Westley's foe would choose incorrectly, and his foe would die and Westley would remain alive.

After a lot of overthinking by Westley's enemy, his enemy finally decides which cup he's going to drink and proceeds to die. Sorry if that spoils the movie for you, but it's been out since 1987, so you've had plenty of time to see it by now.

Westley later reveals that he put poison in both cups, but he had conditioned his body to be immune to small doses of that specific poison. In other words, he had trained his body to live with it.

That's where some of us are with bitterness. We've conditioned ourselves to live with poison, but this isn't the kind of poison that's going to help us win a battle of wits.

Again, having a poisonous root in your heart doesn't seem fair when you may not have committed the offense. It's almost like you have this root in your heart now, but you didn't plant the seed.

However, ignoring the root just because you didn't plant the seed is what keeps you in a cycle of misery.

Bitterness Will Impact Your Health

You may think it doesn't have an effect on your body, but as you tolerate bitterness, you become conditioned to it. Once you become conditioned to bitterness, you only require a stronger dose, and the impact on your life only becomes more evident.

It always amazes me how the Word of God plays out in the physical world, not just the spiritual.

In Deuteronomy and Hebrews, we are warned of bitterness. We are warned of curses and poison, but scientific studies have now confirmed that bitterness has an impact on our physical health.

A study by the Mayo Clinic found that those who held on to unforgiveness and anger, compared to those who regularly forgive and release anger, have:

- worse mental health
- more anxiety, stress, and hostility
- higher blood pressure
- more symptoms of depression
- a weaker immune system
- worsened heart health
- worse self-esteem[1]

God's Word has benefits that translate to your life when honored, and on the flip side, God's Word has consequences for your life when dishonored.

If living in accordance with God's Word isn't enough, come on this journey with me so your physical health improves.

When I told my friend I was writing a book to deal with bitterness, her response was, "Bitterness makes you age. That's my motivation." Maybe we need to market releasing bitterness better.

Releasing bitterness: like Botox but better!

We've learned from the Bible that bitterness brings curses instead of blessings, that it bears bad fruit in our lives, that it is a poison to us, and that it has negative impacts on our health.

That list looks a lot like what you would hope happens to the one who hurt you, doesn't it?

God has made it clear through his Word that, though we may have been the ones wronged, it is our job to get rid of bitterness as fast as possible.

APPLICATION

Where do I have roots of bitterness in my life?

How have those roots of bitterness affected me?

Take time to write a declaration about your commitment to releasing bitterness.

Prayer: *Lord, thank you for showing me how bitterness is impacting my life. I don't want to be bitter. I'm just struggling with what was done to me. Please help me to release bitterness so I can walk in the freedom of forgiveness. I pray that you would be my partner in this and show me where I have roots of bitterness that I need to release so I can live at peace with others and have a pure heart.*

NOTE

[1] Mayo Clinic Staff, "Forgiveness: Letting Go of Grudges and Bitterness," Mayo Clinic, November 22, 2022, https://www.mayoclinic.org/healthy-lifestyle/adult -health/in-depth/forgiveness/art-20047692.

FOUR

"But I Didn't Do Anything WRONG"

Have you ever been blamed for something you didn't do?

In my sophomore year of college, I took a speech class. The semester had just started, and I was relieved that we didn't have assigned seats. I walked into the classroom and sat down next to a friend.

Class began, and meanwhile, my friend got a text that upset her from the guy she was dating. She turned to me and started talking about it. I remember trying to listen to the professor, validate her feelings in short little whispers of "Oh yeah" and "That's hard," and quickly end the conversation so we could pay attention to the lecture.

Before I could ask her if we could talk after class instead, my professor stopped her lecture and turned to us. I still remember her exact verbiage. She said, "I'm sorry, ladies, but if there's something you need to discuss, can you do so outside of the classroom?" Her tone did not reflect that she was sorry. It reflected anger. And she didn't really care who was talking more—we were both deemed the guilty party.

I wanted to jump up and say, "I wasn't the one talking! I was just caught in the conversation!"

Many of us have been there, too. We've been involved in a disagreement, or someone instigated a fight, and we wanted to wear a sign that says, *I didn't start this! I was just caught up in it!*

I've found I'm most susceptible to bitterness when I feel I was not at fault.

It's like when you get cut off in traffic. You didn't do anything other than be there. But someone cut you off and now you're mad.

That's why the hardest thing that life experience has taught me about bitterness is this:

Bitterness doesn't care if you were innocent.

You are susceptible to bitterness even if you are not in the wrong.

Many of us reading this book either think we did nothing wrong, or we think what we did was less wrong, but either way, the trap for bitterness was set the moment someone offended you.

The moment someone wronged you,

The moment someone had something you wanted,

And Satan loves it.

You can be minding your own business, have something done to you, and find yourself bitter.

That's what makes it so deadly.

We saw in the last chapter what Deuteronomy and Hebrews have to say about bitterness. It's poison! It will destroy your life!

The confusion lies in the fact that we don't expect poison and destruction to come upon someone who didn't do anything wrong.

We would certainly expect those consequences for someone who committed a serious sin. We would expect there to be those consequences for the murderer, the adulterer, the fornicator, the liar, the stealer, and the manipulator, but would we expect those consequences for the person who is bitter?

After all, if you're like me, you probably have good reason to be bitter. You were wronged.

Someone took something from you. Someone slandered your name.

Your life was going one way and now it's not because of this person.

It feels unfair that someone innocent is still at risk of reaping the consequences should they choose to befriend bitterness.

Now, suddenly, you find yourself left with hurt and emotions that are somehow your responsibility to deal with, and I'm delivering a message to you that there are consequences if you don't?

Yes.

This further explains why bitterness is one of Satan's greatest weapons.

Among his weapons, you'll find things like temptation, lust, greed, and pride. But you'll notice that all his other weapons require action on your part. They're either your idea, or you choose to give in to them.

Bitterness is different. We didn't choose to experience the pain, but we find ourselves in a position where we have to do something about it.

Bitterness and To-Do Lists

This is a perplexing place to find ourselves in for those of us who seek righteousness.

Psalms 15:1–2 always sticks with me: "O Lord, who shall sojourn in your tent? Who shall dwell on your holy hill? He who walks blamelessly and does what is right and speaks truth in his heart" (esv).

The above list of qualifications goes on in the verses after, but it's that first characteristic that stuck with me.

"He who walks blamelessly . . ."

Many of us strive to walk blamelessly. We know sin keeps us from God, and we do everything we can to get it out of our lives.

We develop a mental checklist that helps us keep tabs on our own righteousness.

But the problem with our checklist is that bitterness never makes the list.

I'm a big to-do list person. I'm the type of person who writes things I've already done on my to-do list just so I can cross them off. Sometimes I'll be in meetings, and as I utter the words "I can do that," I'm simultaneously typing it on my to-do list. I learned that if it's not on my to-do list, I'll likely forget to do it.

As serious as I am about checking off my to-do list, there are some things I don't add to my to-do list. I call them "why bother?" tasks.

It's the stuff that seems so obvious you don't think you need to write it down.

Responding to that text.

RSVP'ing to the event.

Changing the battery in the smoke detector so it doesn't go off at 2 a.m.

It's the kind of stuff that takes about as long to do as it does to write it down on a to-do list. However, that is often the stuff that gets missed. We think we don't need to write it down, and somehow, it's what we forget to do.

Looking at my "righteousness checklist," I see bitterness as the same as those two-second tasks you never add to your list.

When we think of a righteous life, we think of abstaining from sin, but we often don't think about controlling the emotions in our hearts. Particularly when we don't feel we're the one with the issue.

And bitterness? That has the potential to spring up in our hearts and stay there for a long, long time.

A Secure Footing

What do I mean when I say it springs up in your heart and stays there? I'm talking about Satan getting a foothold in your life.

Ephesians 4:26–27 tells us: "'In your anger do not sin': Do not let the sun go down while you are still angry, and do not give the devil a foothold" (NIV).

Personal story time: My husband and I enjoy hiking together. What I should say is that my husband enjoys hiking, and I enjoy taking pictures once we get to the top.

He planned an adventure trip to Acadia National Park in Maine for us to go hiking together. There was a hike on the trip that was referred to as the hardest hike in the park. It was called The Beehive. It was really a hybrid between hiking and rock climbing. Some people had even become injured while climbing The Beehive.

I know this because I look up every possible danger that awaits me before we do our hikes. Need a stat about bear attacks? I got you! Mountain lions? Yup. Moose? Sure thing. Hiking accidents? Yeah. Do I live in fear sometimes? Absolutely. One day I'll write a book on that, but today is not that day.

Given all of that context, I'm not sure how my husband convinced me to do this hike, but he did. This was the steepest hike I had ever done, and when I looked down, I was nauseous. There were several parts when I was shaking while walking across narrow bridges.

As I kept climbing toward the top, I kept checking to see where my feet were positioned. I knew that I could only keep going if my feet were securely positioned.

Do you know the definition of a foothold?

According to the *Oxford English Dictionary*, it means, "To gain a secure position from which further progress may be made."[1]

I knew I couldn't keep going without a foothold.

If the idea of Satan getting a foothold in your life doesn't concern you, think about it this way: the foothold is just the beginning.

The foothold represents the fact that Satan wants to gain ground on your heart and he's now in a position to do it.

Just like I could gain ground on The Beehive hike because of footholds, Satan can gain ground on your life when you give him a foothold.

Don't let him start. Do everything you can to not let him even have a foothold. That's his point of entry!

If you knew someone was trying to break into your house, wouldn't you, at a minimum, lock your front door?

If he can't enter, he can't gain ground. Period.

That's why I feel strongly that we've failed to recognize the seriousness of bitterness.

We may be justified in our hurt.

It may not have been fair.

They may have slandered you, cheated on you, physically hurt you, or taken something from you.

And I am so, so sorry.

I have tears in my eyes as I write this and think about the pain that some of you have experienced without it being any fault of your own.

But, friend, if we give in to bitterness, we are only embracing a lie that Satan is using to gain ground on our heart.

While a lot of circumstances can be breeding grounds for bitterness, I believe there are multiple traps the enemy sets for us that lead to him gaining ground in our hearts.

In other words, there are multiple traps he sets for us that lead to the bitterness root.

That root then settles in our hearts and grows deep within us.

Those traps are offense, jealousy, and unforgiveness. We'll talk briefly about these three, all of which lead to bitterness and give Satan a foothold that he will use to take over your life.

APPLICATION

What have I been using to justify staying bitter?

What timeline will I give myself to release bitterness so the devil does not establish a foothold?

Prayer: *Lord, please help me settle in my heart that I have a part to play in releasing bitterness even when I have lived blamelessly. Please help me have a pure heart so that I may release all bitterness and unforgiveness to the person who wronged me.*

NOTE

[1]Oxford English Dictionary, s.v., "foothold," "foot (n. & int.), c1425–1692," accessed November 15, 2023, https://www.oed.com/search/advanced /Meanings?textTermTexto=foothold&textTermOpto=Definition.

FIVE

"I'm So OFFENDED"

Over twenty years ago, a Canadian man threw his cigarette butt into the grass on his property. As a result, a fire was reported at 1 p.m. that day, and it spread rapidly. The fire department dropped a total of 400,000 liters of retardant and used eighty-seven firefighters, four helicopters, five bulldozers, two excavators, and three water trucks in their fight.

The fire moved quickly at eighty meters per minute. Two days later, the fire had become active on both sides of the river that separated the trees in the Canadian town. The fire became a firestorm by creating its own wind, pulling in more oxygen, and burning hotter. Trees were twisted by the winds as a result. The fire set the local Tolko-Louis Creek sawmill on fire. The mill manager called firefighters to let them know that two one-million liter tanks of propane were located in the sawmill, only fueling the fire as it engulfed the mill.

The fire resulted in the loss of seventy-two houses, nine businesses, 180 jobs, and cost $40 million to extinguish and in property damages. In total, the fire's size was 65,285 acres.

It's amazing how something so small caused so much damage.

In this chapter, we're going to unpack offense. Offense is kind of like a smoking cigarette butt. We'd never believe it could cause that much damage; but in the right environment, it certainly can.

The problem with assuming offense won't cause harm is that offense can lead to some painful feelings and even the loss of relationships if not dealt with.

Before I share some examples, I want to be specific about the type of offense I'm talking about.

The offense I want to focus on fits within this definition: "annoyance or resentment brought about by a perceived insult to or disregard for oneself or one's standards or principles."

In fact, the word *offense* comes from the Latin word *offensus*, which means "annoyance," and *offensa*, which means "a striking against, a hurt, or displeasure."[1]

Doris Kearns Goodwin wrote *Team of Rivals* as a biography on how Abraham Lincoln led his cabinet and the nation through a turbulent time. Throughout the book, she notes that one of Lincoln's greatest leadership traits was his ability to rise above "personal slight," the little verbal jabs or looks—sometimes subtle or not so subtle—designed to hit you on a personal level.[2]

It's the feeling you get when someone says:

"It's great that you don't get lonely even though you've been single for so long."

"Oh, so you're just a stay-at-home mother? That must be so nice to have all that time."

"What a cute little house you have."

"I love that you don't care what people think about your car."

"It's great that you married someone who loves God over marrying someone for their looks."

Offense often feels like someone violated you, but it's different. When someone violates you, they are doing something against you that hurts you, harms you, or impacts you in one way or another, regardless of how you choose to respond.

Offense, on the other hand, typically occurs when you are upset by the way someone perceives you or made you look a certain way to others. I can think of instances when I took offense to something that was unintentional, but it hurt just as much.

Personal story time: I helped start a church plant as the worship team leader seven years ago, and I love visiting other churches to experience their service! I remember visiting another church in the area during their Wednesday night service. At the time, we had only been around for a year or two and were growing slowly but surely.

I had a chance to talk to the pastor of the church I was visiting and told him about my involvement at my church. He said he had a funny story for me regarding my church. He went on to tell me that when we sent our flyer out that said "Welcome home!" (a slogan that a lot of churches have adopted), he had a staff member text him and ask him, "Did this small church just copy us?" since they used that slogan, too.

He was laughing because he told his staff member that they weren't the first church to use that slogan either. I laughed in the moment, but I walked away focused on one word: *small*. His staff member had called us a "small church."

To be fair, we were a small church, as we had only existed a year or two! But I had poured my heart and soul into this church to see it grow to reach more people. I came from attending a megachurch during my time living in Missouri. We saw hundreds of people saved monthly and baptized. It was amazing how God moved.

I so badly wanted what I experienced in Missouri to be my instant reality at my church in Iowa. As I retell that story, however, it's clear to me that no offense was intended by him, and me taking offense only exposed an insecurity that I had.

It doesn't really matter if the offense was or wasn't intended.

It doesn't really matter if the offense was big or small.

It doesn't really matter if you forget about it or remember it five years later.

In all of these circumstances, taking offense is a choice.

Do you ever notice you say you "got offended" or "took offense"? We say the words "got" and "took" as if they're things we acquired. When you come home from the store and someone asks you, "What did you get?" the answer is usually exciting! For me, I usually respond with, "I got a new pair of shoes!" that I'm excited about while my husband is less excited about them.

But how often do we get home from work, church, or even just driving, and the only thing we "got" was offended?

"Well, we didn't like how the pastor phrased that."

"Can you believe how this driver cut me off?"

"Guess how they made me look in front of my boss today?"

It makes me think of those shirts people wear that say, "My daughter went to Clearwater, Florida, and all I got was this T-shirt." Some of us need shirts that say, "I went to the grocery store and all I got was offended."

When someone violates you, they have chosen to do that against you, and you are hurt because of it. If someone kicks you in the shin, they have chosen to violate you, and you may have pain because of it without choosing to accept the pain of the violation. When someone offends you, while your initial feelings are valid, it is ultimately your choice to accept the offense. Just like I chose to get that new pair of shoes, we choose to get offended.

What you take offense in exposes your insecurities.

We can recognize that what offends us most are the things we are insecure about.

For example, I'm perfectly comfortable with someone making fun of my driving because I'm not a great driver and I've never aspired to be a great driver. This is probably not the thing I want to admit in writing, but at this point, we're friends, and we're only going to get closer on this journey, so I might as well share from the heart.

I have, however, taken offense when someone has made fun of my height. I'm of average height, but I have always wanted to be taller and have long, lean legs. Especially since height is a characteristic you're predisposed to and can't change, I have had a hard time in the past when people have made comments about it.

It took me accepting that this is how God made me to be and knowing that he doesn't make mistakes for me to get over my insecurity and be more comfortable in my skin.

Offense Focuses on the Small Rather Than Our Call

There is a good example in the Bible that showcases what happens when we choose to take offense due to our insecurities and when we don't.

David, whom we know as the king of Israel, started out as a shepherd boy. The prophet Samuel was obedient to the Lord and went to the house of David's father, Jesse, to anoint one of his sons as king.

When Samuel first arrived, he saw Eliab, David's oldest brother. In 1 Samuel 16:6, we're told that Samuel thought: "Surely the LORD's anointed stands here before the LORD" (NIV).

But in verse 7 (NIV), God spoke to Samuel by saying:

> Do not consider his appearance or his height, for I have rejected him. The LORD does not look at the things people look at. People look at the outward appearance, but the LORD looks at the heart.

Samuel went on to consider seven of David's brothers and felt that the Lord was not calling any of them to be king. In verse 11, Samuel asked, "Are these all the sons you have?" (NIV). Jesse had an *oops!* moment and mentioned David, his youngest, who was tending to sheep.

Samuel demanded that they send for David, and when he arrived, the Lord confirmed that he was the one to be anointed as king.

We hear that story, and we think of how amazing David must have felt to be anointed king. But I want you to consider a different perspective.

A prophet comes to your house looking for a king and assumes your oldest brother is going to be king because he looks the tallest and strongest.

Then, after all seven of your other siblings are rejected, it takes the prophet asking, "Do you have anyone else I've missed?" for your dad to remember you!

Do you think David could have been offended?

Guys, I'm offended when I'm not invited to a birthday party for a friend of a friend. David could have easily been offended. But David knew what I need to keep learning.

> Those who plan to accomplish big things don't bother with things as small as offense.

David knew he served a big God who had big things in store and chose to dwell on that rather than take offense. He was secure in himself and in God and others, and this played out in every element of his life.

You could say, *Yes, but David was anointed king—why should he have insecurities?* How would you feel if your older brother was called out in the Bible—the infallible Word of God that endures forever—as looking like a king more than you?

Then, to top it all off, one of the most embarrassing moments of your life, when your family forgot to consider you for being king, is something billions of people have read about! David was the youngest brother, and, as you can see from the text, he was often forgotten about or mistreated. It would have been easy for his insecurities to be triggers for taking offense!

Later, David went to take food to his eldest siblings at the battlegrounds where the Israelites were fighting the Philistines. David was going down to check on his brothers when he heard what Goliath was shouting against the Lord.

David was so angered by Goliath defying the Lord that he was emboldened to fight him. Rather than cheer him on or be grateful that his little brother had the courage that he didn't have, Eliab asked David, "Why have you come down here? And with whom did you leave those few sheep in the wilderness?" (1 Sam. 17:28 NIV).

Did you catch that?

Those *few* sheep.

This *small* church.

Eliab suggested that David should not have left the sheep and that his job was insignificant. He was attacking him on all fronts.

Let's pause for a minute. Eliab was the same brother who looked the part of king but wasn't chosen by Samuel. He was the oldest, the strongest, the tallest—you name it, he was it!

I would submit to you that Eliab took offense when he was not anointed king, and jealousy grew in his heart toward his brother David. Now David was here at the battle talking about fighting the giant Eliab was too afraid to fight.

That's where you find him in 1 Samuel 17:28, when he called out that David was tending to a "few sheep" (NIV). It's almost as if Eliab thought that he could control David's destiny or feel better about it if he could continue to minimize him.

While David could have taken offense again, instead, he had the same response in both instances. He focused on what God had for him instead of what others thought of him.

When Samuel arrived to anoint the next king and he wasn't considered, you don't hear of David pouting that they left him out in the field.

When Eliab tried to minimize David's job by pointing out that he only tended to a few sheep, you don't see David get caught up in it.

Rather, both times, he continued with the calling God had for him that day.

Imagine if David had taken offense and run off only to not be anointed by Samuel. Think what would have happened if David had let anger burn in his heart against his brother's offensive words and had gone home instead of focusing on defeating Goliath.

When we choose to take offense over continuing in God's calling, we miss out. We may not see it at the time, and we never know what we missed out on, but we do.

David's potential for taking offense was no greater than the battle we face when we want to take offense. Yet, our persistence to continue in God's calling instead of getting caught up in offense is just as important as David's was. Maybe we aren't slaying literal giants or being anointed as a future king or queen by a prophet, but that doesn't change Satan's tactics. He is trying to get you caught up in offense to keep you from your calling. Who's to say that your calling isn't as great as David's?

Most of us have been like David. We've been in a place where someone has minimized us, intentionally or unintentionally. Here's something to remember: the insult has more to do with the offender than it does with the one offended.

When people unintentionally offend us, it exposes our insecurities. When people intentionally offend us, it exposes their insecurities.

If the insult given was unintentional, as they often are, it could mean that the person was unaware, out of touch, or just human.

If the insult was intentional, then, just like Eliab, it exposes more about the person who gave the offense than the person they meant to offend.

We don't get to choose what the Eliabs of the world say to us, but we do get to choose how we respond. As we talked about earlier, there isn't an expectation that you never feel offended. One of the key steps to forgiveness is validating your feelings rather than excusing the violation or offense. It is okay to be hurt by what someone says or implies. What we need to be careful of is continuously taking offense and holding on to it for long periods of time.

Treat offense like the "hot potato" game, and get rid of it as fast as you can.

Offense Starts Small but Leads to Our Downfall

Not only does what you choose to take offense in expose your insecurities, but it can also expose who you let define you. Many of us have heard the phrase "Live for an audience of one." In other words, live your life as if God is the only one watching and you are solely trying to please him rather than the masses. There are days when I do a great job of this and days when I live for the opinions of everyone. On my worst days, I seek to please even the people whom I've never met and who don't care about me in the slightest.

Many of us are familiar with the story of Esther, a teen girl made queen who saved her people from death thanks to God, her courage, and her cousin, Mordecai. While Esther set the example of living for an audience of one, for the sake of this point, I want to focus on Haman.

Haman was described as the most powerful official in the empire and was thought of as second-in-command to King Xerxes, Esther's husband. The king had commanded that all of his officials would bow down before Haman to show him respect when passing by. Mordecai, Esther's cousin, would not bow down to Haman, and this troubled Haman greatly.

Esther 3:5–6 (NLT) tells us:

> When Haman saw that Mordecai would not bow down
> or show him respect, he was filled with rage. He had
> learned of Mordecai's nationality, so he decided it was
> not enough to lay hands on Mordecai alone. Instead, he
> looked for a way to destroy all the Jews throughout the
> entire empire of Xerxes.

Haman's plot to kill all the Jews had been approved and made public, and he saw Mordecai on his way home from a banquet with the king and Queen Esther. The Bible tells us, "When he saw Mordecai sitting at the palace gate, not standing up or trembling nervously before him, Haman became furious" (Esther 5:9 NLT).

Haman went home and was bragging to friends and family about everything the king had bestowed upon him. He boasted about his wealth, his status, and his promotions. He even boasted about the banquet he was invited to with Queen Esther where she would expose Haman's wickedness. But Esther 5:13 quotes Haman: "But this is all worth nothing as long as I see Mordecai the Jew just sitting there at the palace gate" (NLT).

When I read that, I couldn't help but think: Why? What was it about the acceptance and recognition from this one lowly palace official, Mordecai, that drove Haman's obsession? Haman, after all, had the approval of the masses! He had been exalted by the king! He was second-in-command and had every earthly thing he could have desired except for air-conditioning and a Tesla. But he could not get over the fact that one man was not bowing down to him.

Haman decided to let Mordecai's opinion of him define his worth. Interestingly, if Haman had sought God's approval over both Mordecai's and the masses', he may have pivoted to living a God-honoring life and likely would have won Mordecai's approval as well.

This obsession and hatred led him to propose the annihilation of an entire group of people. Think about that. The offense of one man led to hatred toward an entire group of people, so much so that he was promoting their death.

It seems crazy when you say it out loud, but we're not far off today. How many of us group people by their political affiliation, race, nationality, gender, or otherwise? The offense we take from one person leads us to have negative feelings toward entire groups of people.

In this case, Haman fixated on Mordecai's refusal to bow down, and it led to his own disgraceful death when he was exposed for attacking Queen Esther's people. While this is an extreme example, we cannot miss the point God is showing us: offense exposes who defines you, and it leads to our downfall when we let ourselves be defined by someone other than God.

Offense Starts with "Me" but Turns into "We"

Haman chose to make his offense a dilemma for the entire nation. We're told that in Haman's decree, he offered the land owned by any Jews to whoever killed them. What started as something so small turned into a nation being motivated to adopt his hatred.

How often do we encourage our friends to judge those who have hurt us? I'm sad to admit that there are a number of people I've disliked because they hurt a friend of mine. All too often we can make someone else's offense our own problem.

> Like one who grabs a stray dog by the ears is
> someone who rushes into a quarrel not their own.
> (Prov. 26:17 NIV)

For the dog lovers out there, I'd like to call out that stray dogs in that time were ravenous, wolflike animals. They were not adopted into homes nor were they the kind of dog you'd want to be aggressive with.

Proverbs is reminding us that when we meddle in an argument that isn't our own, we're going to get bit!

I've seen it happen often. One person's offense leads to hatred from a multitude of people, and usually the offense was unintended or misconstrued by the person offended.

In Haman's case, I believe he was killed immediately because he turned offense into "we." In Esther 5:14, Haman's wife, Zeresh, and all his friends encouraged Haman to set up a sharpened pole for Mordecai to be impaled on, and Haman ordered the pole to be set up.

Later, after Queen Esther exposes him to King Xerxes, one of the king's eunuchs reminds the king that a sharpened pole is readily available thanks to Haman's command. The king immediately commands for Haman to be impaled on the pole.

Do you think Haman would have had more time to change the king's mind had the pole not been set up? I do. Haman turned his offense from "me" to "we," and it cost him his life.

How to Stop Taking Offense

David had the approval of few, refused to take offense, and was promoted to king. Haman had the approval of many, including the king, and taking offense led to his death.

But how do we stop taking offense? Sometimes it doesn't feel like a choice when the hurt we experience is real. I'm going to give you three thoughts as you move forward in refusing offense.

1. Assume the Best

I love the quote from Stephen R. Covey that says, "We judge ourselves by our intentions and others by their behavior."[3] Here's the thing about when someone offends: it's often unintentional or unrealized, or it was never meant to be interpreted the way that you took it.

We expect people to give us grace when we offend unintentionally, but it's harder to be quick to release offense when it's done against us.

The Bible tells us in Proverbs 19:11, "It is to one's glory to overlook an offense" (NIV).

I especially like how the New Living Translation puts it: "Sensible people control their temper; they earn respect by overlooking wrongs."

Have you ever had a friend who never gets upset? They are a breath of fresh air. They're the kind of people I want around me all the time. They have my love, and they've earned my respect.

While sometimes we need to have honest conversations if someone's words have hurt us, I would encourage you to be the friend who assumes the best. As we talked through above, it's better for you, and it's better for your relationships!

2. Let God Define You

Just as we saw David be unbothered by Eliab's words, we can choose to put our worth in God rather than others. This one will be the hardest of the two steps, but it will make releasing offense the easiest!

It is hard to offend the person whose self-worth doesn't depend on what you think of them.

There are two ways to stop caring what others think of you:

1. *You can decide that your opinion is the only opinion that matters.*
   This is the wisdom of the world. This route typically leads to a narcissistic view of yourself and over time can lead to mistreatment of others because you have stopped caring for them altogether.
2. *You decide that God's opinion is the only opinion that matters.*
   This is the way God intended us to live. That's why his Word encourages us that we are "fearfully and wonderfully made" (Ps. 139:14 NIV), that we should trust in the Lord with all our hearts and he will direct our paths (Prov. 3:5–6), and that he will provide for our every need (Matt. 6:34).

3. Be a Firefighter, Not a Propane Tank

Just like the fire that started so small, with offense, we need to commit to being firefighters rather than the propane tanks that fueled the fire. As we work through our offenses, let's be careful not to make our offense someone else's problem.

As the body of Christ, let's commit to releasing offense or kindly addressing it with the person who caused the offense rather than going to others. May we also commit to encouraging friends to address their offense and not fuel the fire by gossip, slander, or hatred.

APPLICATION

What are some instances when I've been offended?

What is God trying to teach me through these offenses?

What are some of my insecurities that easily trigger offense (we all have them!)?

What do I need God's help to heal from so I can choose not to take offense in certain areas?

To address offense head-on, pray something like this: *Lord, I know I can take offense at things. Sometimes they are valid, and sometimes I'm probably failing to assume the best. But either way, I recognize that Satan uses offense to turn into much deeper feelings that keep me from living my fullest potential. I renounce the efforts by the enemy to limit my potential through offense! I pray that you would expose instances where I have taken offense unnecessarily and help me move on from them. Help me see future instances where I may be taking offense, and may I find my worth in you and refuse to tolerate offenses, just like King David.*

NOTES

[1] *Oxford Languages*, s.v. "offense," bab.la, accessed November 20, 2023, https://en.bab.la/dictionary/english/offence.

[2] Doris Kearns Goodwin, *Team of Rivals: The Political Genius of Abraham Lincoln* (New York: Simon & Schuster, 2005).

[3] Stephen R. Covey, *The Speed of Trust: The One Thing That Changes Everything* (New York: Free Press, 2006), 13.

SIX

"They Have Something
I DESERVE"

Earlier, we talked about how bitterness is like a root that grows deep within your heart. As we continue talking about things that lead to the root of bitterness, I'd be remiss if I didn't mention jealousy.

The antidote to jealousy may not be forgiveness, but it's no less important to highlight as we try to move forward from the past. Jealousy is like root rot that comes into your heart and affects the good roots within your soul.

Are you familiar with root rot? I became familiar with root rot not too long ago.

I'm on this quest to see if I can keep plants alive. It's become a running joke among friends and family. I want so badly to be able to keep them alive, but inevitably, I mess something up.

You would think if the plants had water and proper sunlight, they'd be happy campers, but there are other factors at play—factors you can't see.

Enter root rot.

Root rot is exactly what it sounds like—the roots of the plant are rotting.

This can occur for two different reasons. Primarily, it occurs because the plant is poorly drained or the soil has been watered too often. It turns out plants need drainage holes. Without them, the soil can become overwatered, which prevents the roots from getting the oxygen they need to live.

To all my fellow HomeGoods shoppers, most of their beautiful pots do not have drainage holes (at least, all the ones I find beautiful!). At this point, I have seven different pots in our house without drainage holes in which plants have died. They all sit empty around the house. I keep buying the pots, though, because they're just so pretty. There's probably a separate sermon in there called "Stop doing the thing you know isn't working and spending all your money," but let's stay focused.

The other reason root rot occurs is when the roots of the plant are weak. They become more susceptible to the fungus in the soil.

I found it interesting that the fungus may be present but dormant for a long time. When the soil has too much water, the spores from the fungus are activated and attack the roots.

Regardless of which reason was causing root rot, I was so caught off guard that I could be doing all the right things to keep my plant alive externally and miss something internally.

It's the same way with jealousy.

We can be doing all the right things externally and not realize that, internally, we are choking out our ability to thrive as we let jealousy creep in like fungus in the soil.

Do you want to know the most obvious symptoms of root rot? "Gradual or quick decline of the plant without an obvious reason."[1]

That's what jealousy causes. A gradual or quick decline of your soul without an obvious reason.

It's an internal struggle that comes from a lack of gratitude and trust that the Lord has great plans for you, in addition to whomever you're jealous of.

In a world where we post our best selves on social media with more filters than a Brita, I believe jealousy is something we've all come to live with. I've found myself jealous of people I've never met whose lives I wouldn't really want if I stopped to think about it.

But I don't stop to think about it. I just keep scrolling. Before we realize it, this jealousy can cause a gradual or quick decline of our souls without an obvious reason.

Let's go back and keep learning about our friend David.

Following his anointing, David had to deal with jealousy from others his whole life, but none more severe than the jealousy King Saul had for David.

Like Haman's offense we talked about in the last chapter, an offense that started out small and turned into deep-rooted bitterness, Saul started out feeling jealous of David, and his jealousy turned into deep-rooted bitterness.

The Bible doesn't tell us that Saul was told of David's anointing to be the next king. It tells us that Samuel wanted to keep that quiet, so it is likely that Saul was unaware. He did, however, see the hand of God on David's life.

After all, David had the courage to defeat Goliath, and he was so successful in all of his other battles that Saul gave him a high rank in the army. Saul likely saw the favor of God on David and thought, *David has something that I should have. I deserve to have that. I'm God's appointed king.*

In 1 Samuel 18, we see that "when the men were returning home after David had killed the Philistine, the women came from all the towns of Israel to meet King Saul with singing and dancing." Their song went like this: "Saul has slain his thousands, and David his tens of thousands" (1 Sam. 18:6–7 NIV).

Oof. Not the kind of thing you want to hear as king.

The Bible tells us, "Saul was very angry [upon hearing this] . . . . 'They have credited David with tens of thousands,' he thought, 'but me with only thousands. What more can he get but the kingdom?' And from that time on Saul kept a close eye on David" (1 Sam. 18: 8–9 NIV).

Jealousy Starts with Comparison

Jealousy is not this random emotion that you feel. It is bred from comparison.

The hard part is you may not have even been the one comparing yourself to someone else. Maybe, like in this instance, someone else compared you to someone, and that sparked the feeling of inferiority.

I remember when I was eighteen, I was going on a school trip to Nashville to compete at a national conference for Future Business Leaders of America (FBLA). One of my friends pointed out that

American Idol was going to be in Nashville during the same three days—right next to our convention!

I decided to audition.

It was an eye-opening process. In the first round, there were almost twenty thousand people. They lined us up, and we had about fifteen seconds to sing in front of local judges. From there, we had two or three more auditions before we would make it to see the celebrity judges.

It's after you've made it through the third audition and before you see the celebrity judges that they interview you to see if you have a story that they want to record.

I was in the room being interviewed by three producers, and another girl was also in the room in a separate interview with another three producers. This girl was stunningly beautiful. I had noticed her earlier, and I wasn't surprised to learn that she had competed in pageants and had won a more distinguished title than I had.

We both were sharing in our separate interviews about how we had been involved in pageants, and one of the producers stopped and said from across the room, "Did I just hear you both compete in pageants?"

"Yes, but our pageant systems don't get along. We're competition," the girl replied.

That was all they needed.

We filmed three hours of B-roll where they had us doing various competitions, including walking the runway (which was just on a ramp at a hotel), lifting and biking in the gym at the hotel, and answering onstage questions.

During that time, she disclosed that she had fake hair, fake eyelashes, and even had veneers for her teeth to ensure they were perfectly white. I didn't even know a full set of fake teeth was an option for college-aged individuals!

But she had them.

I remember latching on to whatever I could to reassure myself that I shouldn't be jealous.

Lauren, she has fake teeth—her beauty isn't real.

But deep down, I was looking at my teeth in the mirror. I was analyzing my smile—maybe I would look better with fake teeth! I was comparing myself to her, and the show was putting us in a position that was encouraging this competition.

I had to swallow my pride even more as I watched her advance to the round in California and I did not.

She got something I deserved, I thought.

Comparison can take many different forms. Maybe you've thought:

How is the girl who mistreated me married and I'm not?

Why did they get that job when they don't work as hard?

Why do they get to have these life experiences and I don't?

Sometimes, comparison is your own thought. Other times, people spark comparison by complimenting someone else.

You don't get to choose where or why feelings of jealousy spring up, but you do get to choose how you respond.

The same was true of Saul. He didn't control what the ladies sang or thought about David's victories, but he could choose his response.

Jealousy Exposes Your Insecurities

When Saul chose to allow the ladies' song to bother him, he chose to focus on David's victories more than his.

David's favor from the Lord, coupled with the fact that others were noticing the favor of the Lord on David's life, drove Saul mad with jealousy.

The jealousy turned to bitterness. In other words, the root rot led to a quick decline without explanation.

The Bible indicates throughout 1 Samuel that Saul was terrified of losing the throne to David and that he was going to do everything in his power to stop it.

Why?

Not because of anything David said or did to Saul. Rather, David's very existence was a threat to Saul. Saul was mad with jealousy. But the Bible indicates that Saul had been involved in things leading to his own demise with or without David's threat.

The Bible tells us Saul had already done things outside the hand of God. It was Saul's actions that prompted the Lord to lead Samuel to David's house to anoint him.

I suggest to you that Saul knew what he had done and was insecure in the fact that David was receiving the favor of the Lord. "Saul was afraid of David, because the LORD was with David but had departed from Saul" (1 Sam. 18:12 NIV).

Sometimes our jealousy is rooted in the fact that we know we're not fulfilling our purpose or destiny. It may even point to the fact that we know we're not walking on God's path or we're not willing to sacrifice to do so.

We're told in 1 Samuel that while David was playing the lyre for Saul, Saul hurled a spear at David in an attempt to kill him. But David eluded him. Twice.

Did you get that? Two times David eluded him.

Saul only had one spear in his hand.

That means Saul threw a spear at David, missed, went to pick it up, and threw it at David again.

No wonder David had killed more men than him—Saul had terrible aim! Just kidding. Back on track.

The intentionality of Saul hurling a spear at David twice should point to just how deep this bitterness root had grown within Saul.

You would think that after he missed the first time, he would have realized what he had done and stopped. Surely, there were others in the palace who tried to get him to stop.

But he didn't.

Have you ever been there? You're jealous of someone and you say something about them to friends. You try to tear them down in a way that appears to be a joke. Maybe you exclude someone or disengage with them on social media.

You know you should handle it better, but you can't. The emotion propels you to keep going.

While this act of rage should have been a wake-up call to Saul, his jealousy of David only grew. It was as if he felt that his jealousy could stop David from becoming king.

Jealousy Works in the Opposite Way

What's interesting is, I believe it was Saul's jealousy that expedited his departure as king of Israel.

This brings us to another reality about jealousy: jealousy does to you what you hope it does to the other person.

Saul was hopeful that he could stop David from becoming king. He was hopeful that he could limit David's successes. There were even times when he sent him to battle knowing it'd be unlikely that David would survive.

But all his attempts fell short of success. They didn't make David any less fit to be king. Rather, they made Saul less fit to be king.

That's what jealousy does in our lives: the games we play, the things we say to reassure ourselves that we're actually superior, the attempts we make to control or diminish the success of others.

It doesn't make them any less wonderful, successful, or worthy.

It makes us less wonderful, successful, and worthy of what God has for us.

Saul's jealousy only catapulted his removal from being king. It did nothing to stop David from becoming king.

If you're like me, you've been in a position where you wonder how or why God can bless someone. It's particularly hard if you wonder why he's blessing someone who hurt you. Talk about puzzling.

We'll talk about this more in the future, but for now I want you to contemplate this: What did David feel after Saul threw spears at him?

Do you think he had questions? Questions like, *When am I going to be king?* Or maybe even, *Will I stay alive to be king?* What about a question like, *How could God keep a man king who is treating me this way?*

He has something I deserve.

Saul thought David had something he deserved, but really, it was the other way around.

Saul had the kingdom. David had a harp.

David deserved to be the next king. Saul did not deserve to stay king. But again, we see David's response set the example for how to handle the hard questions.

Saul, on the other hand, set the example for why we shouldn't allow jealousy in our lives.

There's just one problem: sometimes we still get jealous!

If you have a hard time admitting that, I'll go first. Sometimes I still get jealous! There are a number of things I never knew I wanted until I saw that someone else had them!

How do we handle this?

Two Steps

Jealousy is a complex topic that can have several antidotes. I've found the below two steps to be the best and most immediate antidotes when jealousy creeps in.

1. Find Contentment in What God Is Doing in Your Life

What if Saul had instead focused on the victories the Lord had given him? Conquering thousands of men is no small feat.

Saul reigned as the first king of Israel, and he was just as much appointed by God as David was.

Saul was the most powerful man in the land! He had so much to be thankful for, but he decided to focus on what he didn't have.

We may not be as rich or powerful as Saul, but we still have reasons to be thankful!

Stop right now and write them down!

The Lord revealed this to me in a powerful way: there is someone who has what you want yet wants what you have!

I typed out this revelation and posted it to Instagram. Shortly thereafter, one of my friends who is very disciplined in her workouts and has a large following on Instagram (more than three hundred thousand) commented that she needed that reminder.

She needed that reminder, too? The person who has what I want needed that reminder?

I will say it again: there is someone who has what you want yet wants what you have.

Practicing gratitude is one of the best ways to combat jealousy.

Did you know that scientists found that gratitude and anxiety cannot coexist in the brain? A study by Lau and Cheng published in 2011 showed that, at a neurobiological level, gratitude regulates the sympathetic nervous system. Our sympathetic nervous system is what activates our "fight or flight" response and is linked to anxiety.[2]

As we become more and more thankful, we increase our contentment and decrease our worry.

It is a powerful antidote that will help as you navigate jealousy.

2. Refuse Competition with Your Teammates

David was Saul's teammate. David was a high-ranking army official whom Saul had positioned to fight on behalf of Israel. He should have been very pleased with David's success. It was benefiting the kingdom he reigned!

However, from Saul's perspective, the women's song was saying, *Saul has only slain his thousands, but David has slain ten times as many! Saul is not fit to be king as much as David!*

What if he saw the song as saying, *Saul has slain his thousands* and *David has slain tens of thousands! Israel is favored by the Lord!*

All too often, we see people on our team as competition.

I see this most frequently with other churches. I mentioned earlier that I put my heart and soul into a church plant. Of course, we wanted to grow as fast as possible. There was no limit to how fast we wanted to grow or how many people we wanted to attend.

It was easy to look at other churches and see their successes as our failures.

For some churches, the number of people who received salvation on one Sunday was as many people as we had in attendance.

In other instances, I would hear of churches doing cool things and was tempted to minimize or critique them.

Why?

Those are my teammates! If they win, we win! If they are reaching people for Christ, heaven is becoming more populated! Just like Saul, we can make our teammates our competition. Instead, we need to cheer on our teammates knowing it benefits the whole team!

APPLICATION

When have I recently experienced feelings of jealousy?

What will I choose to be thankful for when I'm tempted to be jealous?

What things has God called me to focus on that I should invest in?

What is one step I can take to combat jealousy (e.g., give someone a genuine compliment who I see as competition, get off social media when jealous thoughts creep in, etc.)?

Let's pray right now: *Dear Lord, you see my heart. You know I am struggling with jealousy. I've had a hard time with people I know who get opportunities I want, and I've been jealous of people I don't know who seemingly have it all together from afar. I have forgotten the good things you've done for me, and I pray you would bring them to mind and allow me to practice gratitude and contentment. Thank you for helping me see others as teammates and not competition. In Jesus's name, amen.*

NOTES

[1] Elite Tree Care, "Root Rot," accessed June 19, 2022, https://elitetreecare.com/library/tree-diseases/root-rot/.

[2] R. W. Lau and S. T. Cheng, "Gratitude Lessens Death Anxiety," *European Journal of Ageing* 8, no. 3 (2011): 169–75; Madhuleena Chowdhury, "The Neuroscience of Gratitude and Effects on the Brain," *Positive Psychology*, April 9, 2019, https://positivepsychology.com/neuroscience-of-gratitude/.

SEVEN

"I Can Wait to FORGIVE"

'm trying to get better at meal prepping. I've found that if I can have meat thawed out in the fridge and ready to go, it helps me whip up a meal. Every Sunday night, I try to lay out a few packages of meat from the freezer.

The only problem is that life happens some weeks. Sometimes I don't realize we had dinner plans one night, or maybe our leftovers last longer than I thought they would.

Inevitably, we end up with chicken that's been sitting in the fridge for a week with a label that reminds me I bought it two months earlier.

Like chicken we intend to use that goes bad, hurt we intend to forgive turns into bitterness before we know it.

The only difference between bitterness and unforgiveness is time.

Bitterness is unforgiveness left to "sit and think" for too long.

We talked earlier about Ephesians 4:26–27 and how you are giving the devil a foothold whenever you wait to forgive, so let's look at it one more time.

This verse tells us, "'Don't sin by letting anger control you.' Don't let the sun go down while you are still angry, for anger gives a foothold to the devil" (NLT).

I'll admit I've been confused by the time restriction of not letting the "sun go down."

Do you think it means you can never go to bed upset? If it does, then I'm in trouble! Do you think it means you have to call the person you're upset with before going to bed? Does it mean every fight you have with your spouse has to be resolved before you can even get some sleep?

I have found that resolving things as quickly as possible is best, even if your argument is centered on something that involves bedtime as the sun is going down—something like, say, the heat being turned up, off, or down, if I were to speak from personal experience.

While resolving things the same day is ideal, I don't think it's demanding that you resolve everything the same day as much as it's warning you that if you don't release it and forgive as fast as possible, it will grow.

It will become the bitterness plant we talked about that we don't want in our heart with our other life-giving roots.

Put another way, the longer you let it sit, the larger the root grows.

The Sneaky One
Maybe you deduced from my last name that I married into a Dutch family. I certainly don't look Dutch, as much as I'd like to.

When I went over to the Netherlands, I bought my husband, Travis, the famous figurine of the little Dutch boy and girl kissing. Naturally, I used a Sharpie to color the girl's hair dark to match mine.

One of the things the Netherlands is famous for is its tulip fields. We were over there in late April, just as they were hitting peak bloom! There were rows and rows of tulips that were stunning! Each row was designated a color. There'd typically be several rows of one color and then more rows of a different color.

Occasionally, you'd look out across five rows of red tulips and see one lone purple tulip planted among the red tulips.

I'm told this happens because it can be hard to tell the bulbs apart to know which color is which. That's not as fun of an explanation, though.

My sister-in-law, Kaitie, made up a story about how this happens. There's a grumpy old man whose life goal is to ruin these perfectly colored tulip fields. He'll sneak onto the fields and he'll sneak into your garden, and in the middle of the night, he'll plant one purple bulb in your field of red tulips!

She named him Deschnegel.

It kind of sounds like "The Sneaky" if we were making up Dutch words. That's what unforgiveness is like in your heart!

You have a wonderful heart full of well-watered roots, like joy, patience, kindness, and more. Then you have a dispute with someone or someone hurts you, and Deschnegel slides in overnight and plants a bulb that looks different from all the others.

Deschnegel comes sneaking in to put something where it doesn't belong.

Of course, it's much more serious than that. Instead of a Dutch guy with a sense of humor and a tulip, it's Satan with a foothold and the intent to destroy your life.

Remember from Chapter Four that a foothold is a secure position from which further progress can be made. That's what's happening with Satan when you harbor unforgiveness.

> It's giving Satan a foothold to advance.

> It's planting a seed that will grow into a root.

> It's advancing and taking root within your heart.

Demonic Wisdom

Perhaps one of the best ways I heard it put was in a sermon by Pastor John Lindell, who stated that bitterness is demonic wisdom.

The Bible tells us, "The fear of the LORD is the beginning of wisdom" (Prov. 9:10 NIV). Scholars also point to the book of Proverbs as a book full of wisdom. Holding on to anger, hurt, and unforgiveness is still a version of wisdom. It's just not God's wisdom; it's demonic wisdom.

As we've talked about before, most people who are bitter have a good reason to be bitter. But having a valid reason to be bitter is not a good enough reason to remain bitter.

Bitterness is the type of thing that will allow Satan to gain ground in your life to destroy it. God's wisdom comes to give life and life abundantly.

But we can know we should forgive and still not know how to. It's not as simple as saying, "I know it's wrong, so I won't do it." If you're reading this book, unforgiveness is probably the reason why. As much as offense and jealousy are strong traps that lead to bitterness, unforgiveness has the most direct correlation.

The Past Hurts

I want to be sure to express that I'm sorry for what happened to you and how you were wronged.

While I've been writing this book, many have shared stories with me of their pain and heartache. Some have shied away from the topic of bitterness, and others have recalled times in their life when they were most bitter.

It was humbling to hear what some have walked through because the experiences that led me to write this book pale in comparison to the pain that they dealt with. There are instances I hear of when I just want to say, "If I were in your shoes, I don't think I could forgive." Yet, I believe the principles God gave me through my experience aren't exclusively for "minor violations."

I believe these principles are for every instance—they just might require a little more repetition.

Friend, hear me when I say the message of this is not that you can't take time to grieve and process.

> It's not to tell you that you need to get over it and move on.
>
> It's not to tell you that you should just excuse it and act like it didn't happen.
>
> Instead, it is to tell you that there comes a point where the unforgiveness hurts you more than what they did to you hurt you.

Just as I shared earlier, I got to a place where my bitterness was holding me back longer than anything they did to me had. Justified as my bitterness may have been, I found a root so deep and so strong, I didn't know how to move on. I was so upset. I was so hurt. I was so angered.

I didn't just let the sun go down on my anger—I let months pass.

It actually started affecting me physically. That's how it works. It's never just spiritual or emotional or physical. They're all linked together.

I went to see a functional medicine specialist who confirmed that my bitterness emotion was affecting my bladder, my stress levels, and my hormones. She explained that quantum physics has confirmed each organ is connected to emotions, and sure enough, my bladder began needing attention shortly after my experience. I'll spare you the details.

It's been years now, and I still have to remind myself of the truths in God's Word when I think back to those days.

Most of this book is based on learnings I felt God impress upon my heart as I walked through that scenario. Minor as it may be to some who have experienced even deeper pain, God used it to teach me about his nature and the reality of the bitterness we allow.

Ultimately, God taught me that bitterness will ruin your life, and Satan loves to start the process of bitterness with unsettled unforgiveness. It may not seem fair, but it is the truth.

How Do We Forgive?

There are many elements of forgiveness that need to be addressed before we find complete healing. That's why each chapter aims to address a different thought that may be keeping you stuck. Each serves to expose the root cause and address it with truth from God's Word.

Just as finding the root cause is complex, so is working through forgiveness. All too often we are told we need to forgive—but never told how. Below are some steps that have helped me. There is more on this in Chapter Fourteen, but I'd encourage you to continue to unpack the complexity of your hurt in the coming chapters before jumping there.

1. Remember the Covenant

In Chapter Three, we talked about how serious bitterness is. I've included a covenant scripture below:

> I am making this covenant with you so that no one among you—no man, woman, clan, or tribe—will turn away from the LORD our God to worship these gods of other nations, and so that no root among you bears bitter and poisonous fruit. (Deut. 29:18 NLT)

The King James Version phrases the last sentence this way: "lest there should be among you a root that beareth gall and wormwood."

Do you want to know what *gall* means?

Gall (noun): "a skin sore caused by chronic irritation"

Gall (verb): "to become sore or worn by rubbing"[1]

It is both a verb and a noun that refers to a sore caused by rubbing repeatedly.

Seeing the word *chafing* in the definition reminds me of when I ran a half-marathon. I'd have to train with Vaseline on my thighs so that I didn't rub my skin too hard with every step.

Swish. Swish. Swish.

The King James Version gives us a word picture of what a root bearing bitterness looks like: repeated rubbing that creates a sore. When we don't forgive, we replay our bitter thoughts over and over. We are creating our own sores from the repetition.

But the King James Version references another word: *wormwood*.

Wormwood: denotes a bitter and poisonous substance, oftentimes referring to intensely bitter woody plants; it is also called absinthe.[2]

Absinthe is a highly alcoholic spirit that is derived from plants, including flowers and leaves of the wormwood plant. It is known as "the green fairy" because it is said to be a highly addictive psychoactive drug and hallucinogen.

Just like when someone drinks absinthe, when you hold on to unforgiveness, your vision gets clouded. You see things that aren't real. They aren't there. You make up stories. You start having pretend arguments that you win every time in your mind with someone who's not really talking to you.

Like King Saul, you start throwing spears at David when he's done nothing wrong. It should come as no surprise that Saul missed hitting David. His bitterness had figuratively put him in a drunken state.

Our bitter thoughts and unforgiveness are only leaving us with chafed thighs and a hallucinating mindset. We must remember the covenant as motivation for the importance of forgiveness.

2. Remember the Call

If you recall from Chapter Five, David refused to take offense. He knew he served a big God who was capable of big things. When we decide to leave unforgiveness untouched, we are laying down our call and exchanging it for bitterness.

David had a large calling on his life and was clear from an early age. I'd imagine few of us were anointed to be king or queen before the age of twenty. You may be struggling to identify what your calling is or if God has called you to something "big." I would suggest we all have a large role to play in the kingdom of God.

Ephesians 4:31 says, "Let all bitterness and wrath and anger and clamor and slander be put away from you, along with all malice" (ESV). I love that Paul didn't just tell us what not to do, but he instructed us what to do instead in the next verse:

> Be kind one to another, tenderhearted, forgiving one
> another, as God in Christ forgave you. (Eph. 4:32 ESV)

If you don't know what big things God is calling you to, Ephesians 4:32 is a good start. God is calling us to be kind to one another.

To live at peace with one another.

To forgive one another.

I believe one of the ways David was able to forgive Saul was through loving his son, Jonathan. In 2 Samuel 9:1, Saul had died, and David was prepared to reign. He asked if there is anyone in Saul's family still alive that he could show kindness to, for Jonathan's sake.

It can be hard to live at peace with the man who sought to take your life. Sometimes, though, God gives us glimpses into people's lives so that we may have grace toward them when they least deserve it. Saul wasn't just a king; Saul was a dad, a husband, and a son.

There have occasionally been people at church whom I disagreed with or felt hurt by, but when I went to serve in the kids ministry and got to love on their sons and daughters, it softened my heart.

When you can't be in relationship with the person who hurt you, remember that we are ultimately called to love. Maybe, like David, you will have an opportunity to love those around them and, in doing so, can offer them a newfound grace.

Your calling is too important to let unforgiveness get in the way.

3. Remember the Cross

Ultimately, we are called to forgive because we have been forgiven. When Jesus suffered death on a cross for our sins, he paved a way so that we might be with him. It was through this act that he can forgive us of our sins and cleanse us from unrighteousness (John 3:17).

Because of what was done for us, God expects us to give the same grace to others.

Matthew 6:14–15 reads, "For if you forgive others their trespasses, your heavenly Father will also forgive you, but if you do not forgive others their trespasses, neither will your Father forgive your trespasses" (ESV).

It will not be easy, but as we reflect on what Christ did for us, my prayer is that you can offer the same grace to others. Let's continue on this journey together so that we can beat bitterness once and for all and find healing.

APPLICATION

What hurt have I been hesitant to forgive?

How have I justified delaying forgiveness?

Which of the three reminders do I need to focus on in order to forgive (covenant, call, cross)?

Pray something like this: *God, I'm sorry. I'm sorry for allowing Satan to distract me from everything you want to do in me and through me. I'm struggling with this scenario. I'm having a hard time with this person. It wasn't fair what happened to me. But I know that you make all things work together for my good. Please be with me as I move forward in forgiveness and walk in your freedom. Bring healing to my life, and help me set the example for others. In Jesus's name, amen.*

NOTES

[1] *Merriam-Webster*, s.v. "gall," accessed November 20, 2023, https://www.merriam-webster.com/dictionary/gall.

[2] "Wormwood," *Insight on the Scriptures*, vol. 2: *Jehovah–Zuzim* (Warwick, NY: Watchtower, 1988), 1210, accessed June 26, 2023, https://wol.jw.org/en/wol/d/r1/lp-e/1200004629.

EIGHT

"If I Don't STICK UP for Myself, No One Will"

When Travis and I were dating, I worked extra hard to show that I would take on his interests as my own. His family enjoys being out in nature and can even identify different birds by their call and features.

I started working hard to notice different birds and learn what I could.

One day, a bird landed on our porch that I had never noticed before. It had a colored stomach, which was different than the typical pigeons we saw. Excited, I called Travis over. "Come quickly, but don't make any sudden movements! You've got to see this bird!"

"Lauren," he said. "That's a robin."

For the record, a robin is one of the most common birds. So much for trying to impress him.

About a year after being married, we moved from our condo into our first house. Our first morning back from vacation, we woke up early to the sound of a tapping against a window.

It was 6 a.m., and the sun had just risen. There had been storms and high winds all week, so my mind started thinking through what the noise could possibly be.

It didn't stop. It was a consistent tapping, almost as if someone was knocking. Was it a grill accessory swinging and hitting the house? Was it a bird feeder blowing against the siding?

Travis got up to check things out, and who did he discover?

Our good friend the robin!

This robin was beating its head against our window repeatedly. I mean, we've all had days where we want to beat our head against a wall, but what could possibly be the reason for this at 6 a.m.?

Based on the hundreds of markings on our window, we concluded this robin had been beating its head against our window the whole week we were on vacation!

Come to find out, this robin had built a nest on our porch, and to protect its nest, it was fighting off . . . its own reflection.

It had mistaken its reflection in our window for an intruder and was beating its head against our window in defense of its nest.

It was then that I realized I had more in common with this robin than I thought.

How many times do we try to defend ourselves and only end up hurting ourselves? We beat our head against an intruder who is only perceived, and it causes damage to our personhood.

You may be thinking, *But my intruder is real!* And while that may be the case, your defense strategy is only hurting yourself.

When you feel attacked, your body has four different types of responses:

1. Fight: respond aggressively and be ready to attack back.
2. Flight: run away from the threat.
3. Freeze: be unable to move or act against the threat.
4. Fawn: bow down or try to make peace to avoid conflict.[1]

When we think of defending ourselves, our mind goes to the "fight" response of the four listed (fight, flight, freeze, or fawn).

That's certainly one of the ways of defense. However, I would suggest that all four are actually defense mechanisms, even if they don't include fighting. We may prefer one over the other, but all four involve our reaction to an attack—our defense.

When we've been wronged, defending ourselves can seem like a good idea, especially if our frustration or bitterness is valid.

Some of my reasons for defending myself in the past have sounded like:

They can't just get away with it.

I want them to know that I know.

If I don't stand up for myself, it means I'm allowing this behavior.

They need to know they can't treat me like that.

I have to fight for myself. No one else will.

But defending myself has only ever led to temporary relief and often long-term regret.

If these responses only hurt us, are we just left defenseless? No, I would suggest we can have a fifth response: faith.

To elaborate, we can have faith that God will be our defender. The Bible tells us this should be our response in defense, and it affirms this defense mechanism with examples throughout the whole book.

Psalms 23 is often used to show that God will be our comforter, but did you know the psalm shows that God is our defender, too? Verse 5 says, "You prepare a feast for me in the presence of my enemies" (NLT).

If you're like me, you've always focused on the "feast" aspect of that scripture. I start thinking about how God is just whipping up some Chick-fil-A for me and preparing a table. I never really focus on the "in the presence of my enemies" element.

But this verse is highlighting God's nature. He is not just preparing a table for us so our hunger will be satisfied. He is preparing a table for us in the presence of our enemies so that we may be justified.

One winter, I found a message waiting for me on Instagram. The message was unkind in nature and involved several accusations. It was meant to target my insecurities and impact my confidence in my speaking and writing.

I was surprised to see that the message had been sent on a major holiday. I was thankful that I hadn't read the message immediately, as I would have let it impact our family's dinner and time together.

When I was telling my counselor about this, she started to smile. She said, "You were feasting on a day an enemy attacked?"

She reminded me of this verse and pointed out that while someone was trying to drag me down, the Lord had allowed me to feast and enjoy time with family. He protected me from seeing the message, and I believe he protected my heart after I read it so I wouldn't give it any weight.

Our God Fights for Us

One of the Hebrew names for God in this passage is *Jehovah Nissi*— or, "our defender."

The first instance I want to look at involves the Israelites in the wilderness. Here is some super fast context, and if you want to dive deeper, you can find more of the story in the book of Exodus.

Moses was born an Israelite who was essentially adopted by an Egyptian princess after his birth mom sent him down a river in a basket to spare his life.

You can't make this stuff up.

After being raised in royalty (with his native people being slaves to that same royal family), he found out that he was an Israelite by birth. After lashing out at one of the Israeli slaves and killing a man, he fled into the wilderness, where he encountered God.

God called him to go back to Egypt to convince Pharaoh to let the Israelites go free from slavery.

After a lengthy series of events that has inspired several movies, Pharaoh agreed to let the Israelites go free.

The Bible tells us in Exodus 13 that when the Israelites left Egypt, God took them the long way through the wilderness to come up against the Red Sea. It's while they were camped near the Red Sea that they saw the Egyptians pursuing them from afar. Pharaoh had changed his mind and regretted letting them go free.

The Bible tells us this is when the Israelites began to complain.

They said things like, "Was it because there were no graves in Egypt that you brought us to the desert to die? What have you done by bringing us out to Egypt? . . . It would have been better for us to serve the Egyptians than to die in the desert!" (Exod. 14:11–12 NIV).

You can imagine how Moses must have felt.

He already felt like the least qualified guy for this job. Now the people he was leading were blaming him for taking their lives, and he wasn't convinced they were wrong!

Do you remember when we talked about how what we choose to take offense to exposes our insecurities? That's where Moses was.

He never thought he could lead. He never felt prepared or called. Now everyone was attacking him, and he had no defense.

Some of us are in a position where the person who wronged us hit us right where it hurts. They cut us at our deepest insecurity or took from us our lifelong dream.

Moses knows how you feel. I imagine he wanted to defend himself, but instead, he turned to God.

In Exodus 14:13–14, Moses responded to the Israelites, "Stand firm and you will see the deliverance the LORD will bring you today. The Egyptians you see today you will never see again. The LORD will fight for you; you need only to be still" (NIV).

Some of us are thinking, *I wish I would never see the person who hurt me again.*

While we'll likely be in settings with our "Egyptians" again, the message is still the same.

You will see the deliverance the Lord will bring you. The Lord will fight for you; you need only to be still.

Be still? Are you crazy?

If I'm Moses, I'm building a boat to cross the Red Sea! *Sorry, God. Thanks for getting us this far, but we've got a problem, and it looks like you didn't have the foresight to get us out of here, so it's time to take matters in my own hands, okay?*

If I'm an Israelite, I'm sharpening my sword. I'm putting on my armor. I'm getting ready to fight for my family.

Too often we read that verse as if their only option was to stay still and trust that God was going to part the Red Sea for them as the Egyptians were pursuing them with chariots and weapons.

They had other options, but they chose to be still.

What does that mean for us?

It means we can choose to have faith as our defense instead of fighting, flighting, freezing, or fawning.

Had the Israelites tried to defend themselves against the Egyptians, they would have ended up in slavery or dead.

When you defend yourself, you're only hurting yourself.

This is not to say that you can't express to the person who hurt you that what they did hurt. It doesn't mean that you need to act like what happened didn't happen. And it certainly doesn't mean you have to be close friends with this person again.

What this speaks to is the position of our heart.

Rather than fighting to defend ourselves, we trust that God is our best course of defense, and we trust him to be the one to make things right.

Our God Brings Justice

Our God is a just God. It can be hard to understand that he is if it feels like we haven't seen justice in our own lives. Justice is a part of human nature. If someone commits a crime in our country, we want to see the criminal penalized and the victim rewarded by our justice system. Our hearts cry for justice.

But the Bible tells us we are made in the image of God (Gen. 1:26–27). In other words, our desire for justice is a part of God's nature as well.

In fact, one of God's names is *Jehovah Hashopet*, which means "the Lord the Judge."[2] Psalm 89:14 (ESV) tells us, "Righteousness and justice are the foundation of your throne; steadfast love and faithfulness go before you."

When you are before a judge, you have decided to let them handle doling out justice. Just like in a courthouse, we can surrender our human tendency to want to get even, and we let God, the judge, correct the score.

The Bible is very clear on this. Romans 12:19 (NIV) reminds us, "Do not take revenge, my dear friends, but leave room for God's wrath, for it is written: 'It is mine to avenge; I will repay,' says the Lord."

Justice is God's job. Let him do it.

When I let God be the one to fight for me, I have never regretted it. It may take longer than I like. It may not look like how I thought. But it has always been better than anything I could do on my own.

I'd like to think Moses would agree. The Israelites were freed from the Egyptians as they crossed the Red Sea. When the Egyptians went after them, Exodus 14 tells us that when the Egyptians followed the Israelites into the sea, God threw the Egyptian army into confusion and jammed the wheels of their chariots so that they couldn't drive.

The Egyptians were even quoted in Exodus 14:25, saying, "Let's get away from the Israelites! The LORD is fighting for them against Egypt!" (NIV).

When God fights for you, your own enemy may even be able to recognize its God!

Our God Delivers

The second instance we'll look at is when Shadrach, Meshach, and Abednego refused to bow down before King Nebuchadnezzar's idol in Daniel 3. The king threatened to throw them in the blazing furnace if they did not bow down, and he even mocked God by asking, "What god will be able to rescue you from my hand?" (Dan. 3:15 NIV).

Their response to him in verses 16–18 (NIV) is one I hold dear:

> King Nebuchadnezzar, we do not need to defend ourselves before you in this matter. If we are thrown into the blazing furnace, the God we serve is able to deliver us from it, and he will deliver us from Your Majesty's hand. But even if he does not, we want you to know, Your Majesty, that we will not serve your gods or worship the image of gold you have set up.

Whoa. They were determined to let God be their defender even at the risk of it costing them their own lives.

This is true surrender.

Surrender is hard to do when you feel you have something to gain.

Surrender is even harder to do when you feel you have
something to lose.

That's what makes surrendering to God amid an attack so difficult.

You feel that, by letting God fight for you, you may lose
your vindication.

You may wonder, *If I let God fight for me, how will I ever
get justice?*

Just like with the examples we saw in the Bible, God's justice is
better than any justice you could serve up yourself. And how did
God serve justice for Shadrach, Meshach, and Abednego?

The Bible says that King Nebuchadnezzar was furious at their
response and ordered the furnace to be made seven times hotter.
The men who went to throw them into the furnace died just from
being close to the heat.

But Daniel 3:24–30 tells us that the king leapt to his feet and asked
if three men were thrown into the fire. His advisers confirmed that
three men were thrown in. The king was shocked because he saw
four men walking about "unbound and unharmed, and the fourth
looks like a son of the gods" (Dan. 3:25 NIV).

King Nebuchadnezzar shouted for Shadrach, Meshach, and
Abednego to come out of the furnace. When they did, not a hair
on their heads was singed. Everyone who has used a curling iron
knows just how amazing this is. But the Bible tells us they didn't
even smell like fire (Dan. 3:27). And I love what the king said
in response:

> Then Nebuchadnezzar said, "Praise be to the God of
> Shadrach, Meshach and Abednego, who has sent his
> angel and rescued his servants! They trusted in him and

> defied the king's command and were willing to give up
> their lives rather than serve or worship any god except
> their own God. Therefore I decree that the people of any
> nation or language who say anything against the God
> of Shadrach, Meshach and Abednego be cut into pieces
> and their houses be turned into piles of rubble, for no
> other god can save in this way." Then the king promoted
> Shadrach, Meshach and Abednego in the province of
> Babylon. (Dan. 3:28–30 NIV)

That's the God we serve! They were engulfed in flames, and they didn't even smell like a bonfire. The very man who ordered that they be thrown into the fire was the one who promoted them within his kingdom. Our God is a God who delivers.

No Other God Can Save in This Way

When you let God defend you, God is glorified, and you are vindicated.

Years ago, I helped start a church. I remember feeling called back to Des Moines, Iowa, but I didn't know where I should go to church. Through a series of divine appointments, I found out that our family friend was moving back to start a church there the same year I was moving back.

I had a talk with him and told him I'd be happy to serve in the worship ministry if he needed someone, and I would send him some contacts for people I thought would be good candidates to be worship pastor.

A few months into preparation to launch the church, he indicated that I would be the worship pastor. Even though I couldn't tell the difference between an electric and bass guitar, I said I was happy to help however needed.

I spent seven years serving as a worship pastor in a volunteer position while also working at my corporate job. Those were some of the most formidable years of my life. They have shaped my leadership to this day.

Given the growth that occurred, I'll be the first to admit that I was not a strong leader when I started at the age of twenty-three. Not only did I not have the musical background I should have had to lead a band, but I lacked the confidence and ability to lead a team.

There were people on the team who questioned why I was in the position I was in and were vocal about their doubts to the rest of the team. To be fair, even I was questioning why I was in the position I was in. I was trying to be obedient, but I was underqualified and inexperienced.

Most of the team started either resenting me or doubting me. In one day, we lost three-fourths of the team to go help start another church. I felt that I had failed as a leader. At a minimum, I failed by allowing a culture where disunity was tolerated, and I was seeing the impacts.

I badly wanted to defend myself. Much of what was circulating about me was untrue or exaggerated, and few people knew my side of the story.

Instead of fight, flight, fawn, or freeze, I chose faith. I'm not sure I chose faith because I was that wise or that holy. I think I chose faith because I didn't know where else to go.

And just like God defended those in the Bible, he defended me.

Just one of the ways I saw this was through a text message I received five years after this occurred. My dear friend, who at the time disliked me, wrote me to apologize and thank me for my hard work. He said he painted a picture of me back then and allowed himself to believe things that weren't true.

I was not a perfect leader. I didn't deserve all of his kind words. But I didn't have to fight for myself. God did it instead. Because I let God fight for me, he corrected misperceptions my friend had about me and allowed him to offer grace to me as well. Had I fought by myself, I don't believe I ever would have seen that friendship where it is today, and I would have missed out on what God wanted to do.

That story reminds me that I would rather put my trust and hope in my God than myself any day. Sometimes we just need to remember that when our emotions are getting the best of us.

I hope I've convinced you to let God be your defender, even if the other person doesn't deserve it. Here are two tips for how to let God be your defender:

1. Humble Yourself

When attacked, you have a choice of how you're defended and who defends you. But you must make the choice. Will you fight to defend yourself, or will you let God defend you?

At the end of the day, the urge to defend ourselves is usually rooted in pride.

We've probably said something like, *I'm just going to take matters into my hands since I'm not sure where you are right now.* We pick up our armor and begin to fight while thinking things like:

They can't say that about me.

They're going to pay for this.

I'm going to make them regret how they treated me.

But in my experience, when God sees you defending yourself, his response isn't to swoop in and try to outdo you or prove himself.

He's God. He doesn't need to prove himself. When God sees you defending yourself, his response is usually, *Oh, okay, you've got this then. I'll let you try.*

"So humble yourselves under the mighty power of God, and at the right time he will lift you up in honor," says 1 Peter 5:6 (NLT).

We can apply that truth to our situation. We can trust that God will move in his power and in his way. And we can be certain that, in his time, he will lift us up. We humble ourselves under him, and we watch him lift us up.

When we humble ourselves, we say something like, *God, I'm done fighting. I don't care what it looks like. I don't care how long it takes. I'm going to let you fight my battles.*

That's when God says, "Finally." And get ready, because he has never lost a battle.

2. Worship While You're Waiting

Remember when I said that God will fight for us, but we don't get to choose the timing or what it will look like? This is one of the hardest parts about letting God be the one who defends you.

You have to decide what you're going to do while waiting.

During the waiting period, you'll likely be tempted to defend yourself time and time again. As the waiting gets longer, the temptation to defend yourself will become stronger.

I love the lesson we can learn from the Israelites when David wrote: "In you our ancestors put their trust; they trusted and you delivered them. To you they cried out and were saved; in you they trusted and were not put to shame" (Ps. 22:4–5 NIV).

Just like the Israelites learned at the Red Sea, we can put our trust in the fact that God will deliver us and we will never be put to shame. Rather than growing weary in the waiting, one of the best ways to fill your time while you're waiting is to worship.

I love the way Rita Springer wrote it in her song "Defender":

> "All I did was praise, all I did was worship, all I did was bow down, all I did was stay still."[3]

This is the perfect instruction for our response as we're waiting. Counterintuitive as it may seem, all you need to do is stay still.

 **APPLICATION**

Here's a little space for you to write what you need to release to God as you wait for him to defend you:

Here's some space to write a few action steps for how you're going to handle letting God fight for you:

Prayer: *Lord, I know how badly I want to fight for myself. I know the world tells me I should. I know sometimes even my mentors recommend fighting for myself. But I know that if I trust in you and wait on you that you will never let me be put to shame. Help me to humble myself under your mighty hand so that justice may occur and you may get the glory. In Jesus's name, amen!*

NOTES

[1] Olivia Guy-Evans, "Fight, Flight, Freeze, or Fawn Response," Simply Psychology, updated November 9, 2023, https://www.simplypsychology.org /fight-flight-freeze-fawn.html.

[2] Tony Evans, "Praying (and Pronouncing) the Names of God, Page 2," *Tony Evans* (blog), accessed November 6, 2023, https://tonyevans.org/praying-and -pronouncing-the-names-of-god-2022-page-2/.

[3] Rita Springer, "Defender," track 4 on *Battles*, Gateway Create Publishing, 2017.

NINE

"They TOOK Something from Me"

Often, it's not just the pain of the hurt that we have to work through when we are wronged by someone. It's also the loss of something that we have to work through.

Some of us reading this book lost:

- A marriage
- A significant relationship
- Something financially
- A reputation
- Trust with someone close

These losses occurred because of a wrong or wrongs.

Several times, I have lost significant relationships in my life. Every time, the people involved were Christians who loved God, but they had hurt me by their actions or words.

It's always a tough pill to swallow.

There have been other instances that involved attacks on my integrity or purity and rumors spread about me. It's hard to lose something at the hands of someone else. It's especially hard when it feels intentional.

There were times where I hadn't just lost a relationship; I feared losing my reputation and future friends. I didn't know who I could trust, and I felt alone. I had lost my community.

Maybe your greatest losses have also been relationships, or maybe there are other things that have been more painful to lose.

Perhaps someone took something from you financially. Maybe someone took a job from you or took an opportunity from you that you felt you deserved. Typically, whatever loss hurts the most shows us what we value the most.

Some of us didn't just lose one thing when someone hurt us—we lost multiple things. Maybe you didn't just lose your spouse, but you also lost your home, your finances, your comfort, your lifestyle, and your future.

That's why we need to address this thought: *They took something from me.*

This is going to be one of those thoughts that I'm not out to disprove or debunk.

Let's look at a practical example. Imagine me trying to tell someone who had their car stolen that they didn't really have something taken from them.

It doesn't hold up. No matter how I try to comfort you, you still don't have a means of transportation.

Rather than tell you that whoever wronged you didn't really take something away from you, I'd rather give you hope for restoration of what was taken from you.

I would rather give you hope that looks like this: God can restore anything that people have taken from you.

Of course, when we hear something like that, our first response is skepticism.

Many of us have wanted to have this kind of faith, but we have yet to see God restore the thing another person took away from us.

Some of us have had that kind of faith for years until the pain was too great and we became cynical. Let me tell you, friend—I have been there.

But if our faith is contingent upon God doing the specific thing we want him to do for us, we've got it backward. That's why I want to build our faith back up.

Here are the messages we're going to unpack in this chapter:

- God is a good God who delights in every detail of your life.
- God wants to restore, and he has the authority to do that.
- Just because you can't see it doesn't mean it's not coming.

God Is a Good God Who Delights in Every Detail of Your Life

The psalmist says:

> The LORD directs the steps of the godly.
> He delights in every detail of their lives.
> Though they stumble, they will never fall,
> For the LORD holds them by the hand. (Ps. 37:23–24 NLT)

The heart of my reason for believing that God wouldn't restore what I had lost was because I believed the lie that he didn't care about the details. Maybe you're there too. You think:

God doesn't see me.

He doesn't understand.

Or maybe you believe that you're in this position because of something you've done, and God is laughing at you. While I've had those thoughts, I'm here to tell you they couldn't be further from the truth.

Again, the psalmist says, "For you created my inmost being; you knit me together in my mother's womb" (Ps. 139:13 NIV).

At times, Scripture can be poetic. Just like is done in modern-day books, the authors of the Bible used poetry to depict a message. It'd be easy to see this verse and think, *God made me in my mother's womb.* But what's cool about God is, there are lots of hidden secrets in his Word that science later confirms. This verse is one of them.

There are structures in our bodies called microtubules. Stay with me, okay?

Microtubules are responsible for holding your cells together. Virtually all of your cells' movement is conducted by cytoskeletal polymers, of which microtubules are a part. They help the cell grow, divide, and move.

When you view microtubules under a microscope, they look just like a string. In fact, they look like threads wrapped around threads, which create a cord. Actually, almost all of our biological anatomy resembles two intertwined strings if you view it under the right microscope. Here's an illustration:[1]

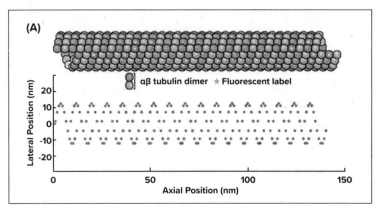

Figure 9.1. Simulation of a Microtubule Image

Pretty amazing how it resembles a thread! Furthermore, a microtubule's diameter is twenty-four nanometers wide. Do you want to know how many nanometers make up an inch? A total of 25,400,000 nanometers.

That certainly gives a new meaning to the thought that God delights in every detail—he knit every detail! Even the smallest ones.

A few years ago, I really got into knitting. I would sit on the couch after work with big chunky yarn and my knitting needles. I'd turn on the fireplace and a show I wanted to watch, and I would go to town knitting.

Although I loved knitting, I wasn't very good at it. I would have pieces of yarn that I didn't pull tightly enough, and I could never really figure out how to finish a piece, which resulted in really long scarves until my friend came over and helped me tie these fancy knots to finish the accessory.

Mediocre as I was, I'll tell you something about the items I knit— I'm never getting rid of them. They're my handiwork. I made them. I can't get over them. I wear them with pride.

Just as we knit strings together to make a scarf, pot holder, or clothing item, biology confirms the concept that God physically knit us together as he created us.

Wouldn't it be cool if when we get to heaven, we'll see God sitting on his throne knitting? Not because he's being passive or because he's weak or because he's more like our grandma than we thought. No, we'll see him delighting in every detail of our lives, which began when he created us in our mother's womb.

Furthermore, the Bible confirms that God desires to give us the best gift of all. This is a gift that has the power to transform your life!

One of my best friends gives the best gifts every Christmas. It doesn't matter what I get her or how much I spend—she's going to top it.

Last year at Christmas, she gave me a nail polish kit I had been wanting with eight different shades, plus socks, a face mask, chocolate, and a sweatshirt because she claimed it "didn't look good on her."

I got her shimmer powder. I even used a discount code she had found to purchase it at a better price.

I really don't know why she's friends with me.

While everything that my friend gifts me is incredible, the Bible tells us that God wants to give us the gift of the Holy Spirit. Jesus told his disciples:

> You fathers—if your children ask for a fish, do you give
> them a snake instead? Or if they ask for an egg, do you
> give them a scorpion? Of course not! So if you sinful
> people know how to give good gifts to your children,

how much more will your heavenly Father give the Holy
Spirit to those who ask him. (Luke 11:11–13 NLT)

You may be thinking, *What does that gift get me?* Think of the
Holy Spirit as a best friend who is a superhero. Are you feeling
alone? Do you need comfort? The Holy Spirit is there. Do you
need wisdom and discernment to know what to do in a situation?
The Holy Spirit can guide you.

Do you need protection when you're traveling, driving, or in situations when you might put your foot in your mouth? Yup. The
Bible says the Holy Spirit will do that, too (Ps. 121:8 NIV).

When I say that God is a good God who delights in every detail
of your life, I mean that God is the God who wants you to have
access to his power, comfort, and insights on a daily basis! He's
concerned with the details so much that he's given us the gift of
his presence, his very essence, his toolbox.

You know when you have a really good item that everyone wants
to borrow? Like a truck for moving, a YETI cooler during the
summer, or a nice curling iron? If I ever loan this stuff out, it
always comes with the disclaimer: "I'll need it back by tomorrow."

God isn't like that. He gives us the Holy Spirit for us to have full
access to his toolbox all the time. All we need to do is ask.

When you feel like someone took something from you beyond
what you can bear, remember that God is a good God who delights
in every detail of your life. Even down to your microtubules.

God Has the Authority to Restore

When I was in high school, nothing was more important to me
than an activity called show choir.

Show choir was an activity where a group of fifty students sang and danced their hearts out to create a twenty-minute show that would have even the most musically averse people going *Whoa*.

The high school I attended had ranked nationally in show choir competitions, and we were repeatedly one of the best schools in the state. I had been involved since middle school and wanted nothing more than to be a part of the varsity group. There had only been two girls to ever make the varsity group as sophomores.

The spring of my freshman year, our music director talked to us about what the next year of show choir would look like. I still remember when he said, "There will be freshman girls in this room making varsity next year."

I didn't think I could wait until the day the varsity group was announced. After my last class, I jumped out of my seat and ran down to the choir room to see the list posted. People already at the list were smiling at me! *Is this really happening? Did I make it?*

I looked and saw my name on the list! I was overjoyed! I went home on cloud nine. And summer ensued.

That summer, things changed.

My sister was in her junior year and looking at colleges, and I was obsessed with the worship band Hillsong United.

When I found out that Hillsong United was going to be doing a concert in the same city that my sister wanted to go to for a college visit, I began to plan the trip!

While there, we stayed with family friends who mentioned a job opportunity to my dad. It was in Springfield, Missouri—the city we were in for the concert—on the trip that was my idea in the first place.

After an interview process, my parents made the prayerful decision to accept the job and move our family to Springfield. That decision rendered all my hard work and excitement around making the varsity show choir group worthless.

What was even more perplexing was that I thought God was the one who gave me the show choir opportunity in the first place! I remember thanking him after I had made it, too! *Well, thanks for nothing!* Didn't he know what this meant for me?

What did I do? How did my determination to go see a band lead to such a huge change for my life?

Throughout this whole book, we've talked about being bitter toward the person who hurt us. And here, instead, I found myself in a place where I was bitter toward God.

I remember people encouraging me that God had a plan. But I couldn't see it.

God, where are you in all of this? was one of my most common questions.

Despite feeling like I had lost everything, God restored everything I lost from that move one-hundred-fold. Instead of show choir, I was able to participate in musicals and plays at a school that had people from Broadway as alums and whom I eventually got to meet!

Instead of singing and dancing with a group of people, God opened doors for me to be a part of productions through the Miss America organization!

If I were to list all the ways God restored my loss, you wouldn't believe it, and you'd probably get bored reading this chapter. The part that amazes me about all of this is that God restored things for me even when I had a bad attitude toward him.

Sure, I learned to trust. I learned to lean on God because he and my family were truly all I had. But that doesn't mean I always did it willingly.

God restored what I had lost because the nature of God isn't determined by who you are. It is determined by who he is.

Let me say that again.

The nature of God isn't determined by who you are. It is determined by who he is.

God's character doesn't change with your actions.

God is the restorer of all things. God is all-powerful to do so. There is nothing that can thwart the plan of God. Our God is the God who restores. And he doesn't just work in the details of our personal lives. Our God works on a broad level as well.

About twenty miles southwest of the city I was raised in, there is a four-hundred-acre piece of property. This property sits across two towns and encompasses rolling hills, large trees, and a large lake. Tragically, the previous owner of the property would bring young men onto the property with the purpose of taking advantage of them.

I can only imagine the pain and the hurt that took place on that property.

When the news broke out, they arrested the man and confiscated the property. Few people wanted the land. It was in the middle of nowhere and had a tarnished reputation. But our God is the God who restores.

A prominent businessman in the state of Iowa was approached to buy this property and turn it into a refuge for children who have been abused or are in at-risk situations. He felt God tug on his heart, and he purchased it.

Years later, Wildwood Hills Ranch of Iowa is a thriving program for kids across the state of Iowa. Wildwood makes a ten-year commitment to each kid who is welcomed onto the property, with the purpose being that they walk alongside them until they are eighteen years old.

Kids who are in situations in which they are at high risk of abuse, whether physically, emotionally, or sexually, are able to come to the ranch each summer and experience peace, joy, and the love of Christ.

Each summer, they serve almost one thousand kids, many of whom accept Christ in their hearts. They continue to engage with the students throughout the school year and are instrumental in plugging them into a network to find jobs and set them up for success for the rest of their life.

The property that once was made famous for the abuse that took place now serves as a refuge for kids who have experienced abuse.

We serve a God who restores.

You may be thinking, *Yes, but that's about a property.*

No, it's not.

The property is simply a tool that God uses to restore lives of children who have had things taken from them.

He'll do the same for you.

We serve the God of this universe. There is no one like him and no one besides him. There is nothing he cannot do, and there is nothing that is outside his hand. All authority in heaven and earth is his.

God wants to restore, and he's more powerful than the person who took something from you.

Just Because You Can't See It Doesn't Mean It's Not Coming

Remember when we talked about how God's character isn't determined by your actions? Our actions do not change who God is. And I'm so very thankful for that.

If our actions don't change who God is, do we still need to have faith or is it just luck? Well, it's a "both/and." God moves in spite of us, and he moves on behalf of us! We learn from examples in the Bible that our faith *can* move the heart of God. It's time to talk about Job.

You may have predicted we'd discuss the life of Job. He's one of the characters in the Bible who had perhaps the most taken away from him for doing nothing wrong. The book of Job is forty-two chapters of pure gold, but since I'm not going to quote it line by line, below is the condensed version.

Satan went to God one day, and they had a conversation. God started bragging on Job and called him "a blameless and upright" man (Job 1:1 NIV).

Satan rebutted by saying it was just because God had blessed him and put protection around him so Satan couldn't hurt him. He argued that if God were to remove his favor from Job's life, Job would curse God.

God agreed to remove his favor and protection from Job's life, but on the condition that Satan could not hurt Job physically.

Trial after trial came upon Job. Satan began to wreak havoc on Job's life.

First, one of his workers came to him to tell him that his workers, donkeys, and oxen had been taken captive by an enemy. Then, another worker came and shared that the workers and the sheep they had out in the field were burned up by fire.

A third worker came and shared that another enemy stole Job's camels and struck down all the workers. Last, a worker ran up to Job and gave him the news that a great wind struck the house that his children were in, and they perished.

What most of us couldn't handle in a lifetime, Job had thrust upon him in a moment.

Job's response is shocking.

> "Naked I came from my mother's womb, and naked shall I return. The LORD gave, and the LORD has taken away; blessed be the name of the LORD." In all this Job did not sin or charge God with wrong. (Job 1:21–22 ESV)

Again, Satan approached God, and God began to brag about Job. Satan claimed it was only because Job himself was not in physical pain that Job hadn't cursed God. The Lord agreed to let Satan attack Job physically, on the condition that he spare Job's life.

Job later had sores across his body from the bottoms of his feet to the top of his head.

"Curse God and die!" Job's wife provoked him (Job 2:9 ESV).

Job's response is, once again, shocking.

> You speak as one of the foolish women would speak.
> Shall we receive good from God, and shall we not
> receive evil? (Job 2:10 ESV)

It got to a point where every person in Job's life was telling him to curse God, but Job wouldn't do it.

Job had everything taken from him. He didn't understand. He didn't do anything to deserve it. Yet it was all gone.

Maybe you're in a place like that today. You feel you've had everything taken from you.

You don't understand it. You don't deserve it. And that doesn't change your reality.

Without suggesting that the person who wronged you is comparable to Satan, I want you to glean from this story Job's outlook in the midst of pain.

The book of Job is a roller coaster of emotions, and rightfully so.

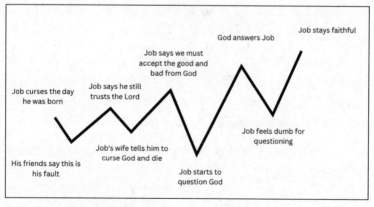

Figure 9.2. Job's Emotional Roller Coaster

Job went through a gamut of emotions. He wondered what he did to deserve this, he thought it would be better if he were dead, and he kept hoping in God.

It goes on for thirty-five chapters of this roller coaster, going from despair and discouragement to determination not to blame God.

Finally, after a lot of questioning, God answered:

> Who is this that obscures my plans with words without knowledge? Brace yourself like a man; I will question you and you shall answer me.
>
> Where were you when I laid the earth's foundation? Tell me, if you understand. Who marked off its dimensions? Surely you know! . . . On what were its footings set, or who laid its cornerstone—while the morning stars sang together and all the angels shouted for joy? (Job 38:2–7 NIV)

These questions continue through the whole chapter.

Some of my favorite questions are:

"Have you ever given orders to the morning?" (Job 38:12 NIV)

"Does the rain have a father?" (Job 38:28 NIV)

"Can you loosen Orion's belt?" (Job 38:31 NIV)

"Do you send the lightning bolts on their way?" (Job 38:35 NIV)

God sent a line of questions toward Job that he knew Job could not answer. Why did God do that? Wasn't this the God of mercy? The God of love? Wasn't God saddened that Job was here in the first place?

Yes, yes, and yes to all the questions!

But God recognized that if Job was going to get out of this, it would take him realizing who is on the throne and resting in him.

Even amid the questioning and the doubt and the pain, Job was being subjected to pain for reasons he couldn't understand. But that didn't make God any less at work.

We need to trust that God is working for our future even when we don't understand it.

I like to put it this way:

> If you believe that there are parts of your future you don't know, then know that there will be parts of your present you don't understand.

God still had a future for Job. And it didn't matter what Satan had taken from him—his future was in God's hands. No pain, scheme, or act of man changed that.

God restored unto Job everything he had lost. And not only that.

Job 42:10 tells us, "The LORD gave Job twice as much as he had before" (ESV).

If you are struggling to forgive the person who has wronged you, I ask you this: Are you confident God can restore what they took from you?

Job 42:11 tells us that his friends came to his house after Job's trials were over to celebrate. While there, they told him how sorry they were, and they comforted him for what he had faced. Even though God gave Job twice what he had before, Job still had sadness in his heart for what was lost. He still lost his children, he may have lost his first wife, and I'm sure there were many favorites Job had that he lost. All those things he would recall for the rest of his life.

Perhaps you're in a similar place where, even if God multiplies what you had before, you will still mourn the loss of what was taken from you. My mind goes to people who have been abused physically, sexually, or emotionally. Maybe you were married before, and through divorce, they took a number of your "first" experiences with them. It could be that someone caused an accident and, with it, physical ailments that you struggle with daily.

Those are the kind of losses where restoration seems impossible. That's where faith comes into play. Restoration doesn't always look like how we want it to. I'd like to think Job would have wanted God to raise his children from the dead to be fully restored. Many of us probably wish we never would have gone through our painful situation or, perhaps, that we never would have met the person who hurt us.

No, restoration doesn't always look like how we want it to. But when we choose to have faith beyond what we can see, God, in his infinite glory, works on our behalf so that the latter can be greater than the former.

One of the best cures for bitterness is recognizing that we serve a God who is bigger than what they did to you. When you wholeheartedly trust in God to restore you and believe that he is in control, you're less bothered by what people attempted to take from you.

Dear friend, hang on! Don't give up now. Now is not the time to give up on God.

You may not be able to see it, but God is on the throne.

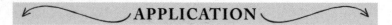

APPLICATION

Let's take a little time and reflect:

What loss am I praying for God to restore?

What action step do I need to take to remind myself that God is in control when I start to doubt?

Scripture to meditate on: "The LORD is for me, so I will have no fear. What can mere people do to me?" (Ps. 118:6 NLT).

Prayer: *Lord, you see what I've lost. You see my brokenness and my pain from this situation (name your situation specifically to him). God, I pray that you would remind me you are the God who restores. No matter what was taken from me, I will look on the days ahead knowing that you can and will restore them. I pray that the days ahead are better than the days behind, and I trust that you will restore all I have lost.*

NOTE

[1] From G. Bohner, Nils Gustafsson, Nic Cade, Sebastian Paul Maurer, Lewis D. Griffin, and T. Surrey, "Important Factors Determining the Nanoscale Tracking Precision of Dynamic Microtubule Ends," *Journal of Microscopy* 261, no. 1 (Oct. 2015): 1–13, here 3.

TEN

"I Want to HURT Them Like They Hurt Me"

*D*on't get mad. Get even.

Have you ever heard this phrase? Many people in society today consider revenge to be a justified next step when someone wrongs them.

Do you know that the Bible says humans are made in the image of God?

That can mean that we have the same desires as God. I'm not talking about our sinful desires. I'm talking about our desire to be loved, respected, and admired. There is also, of course, the desire for justice to be done.

None of these desires are bad; they're often just misplaced.

Our desire to be loved can turn into giving ourselves away for attention.

Our desire to be respected can turn into thirst for power and the mistreatment of others.

Our desire for justice can turn into the temptation to bring about justice for ourselves.

If we're going to heal fully, we must release the desire to bring about justice for ourselves or the desire to get revenge.

Sometimes that can look like acting out in defense, like what we talked about earlier. But the desire to get even goes beyond just defending ourselves.

Sometimes we don't even have to be the ones to get even; we just delight in them feeling pain because they made us feel pain. The interesting thing about seeking revenge is that revenge does not always mean wanting the person to get exactly what you got.

If someone stole from you, you may or may not care that they lose what you lost.

If someone cheated on you, you may want someone to cheat on them, but that may not be enough.

If someone spoke ill of you, you may hope someone speaks ill about them, but that probably won't cut it, either.

No, revenge often involves wanting the person to feel what you felt rather than just get what you got.

You want the other person to understand the pain they caused you and be sorry for it. But that's typically not all. Whatever pain they caused you, you want them to feel, too.

The catch-22 about this is, when you strive to get even, often you become at fault. Then, your enemy has something against you! In your attempt to settle the score, you only evened it. This makes the scoreboard read one to one in terms of wrongdoing.

It's a temporary fix that only leads to more pain. And that's what revenge by our own hands causes: pain.

But that's not the only thing revenge does.

Revenge Holds You Back from Pursuing Your Calling

Whether you love superhero movies or not, when I say *Spider-Man 3*, you may be perplexed at which movie I'm talking about.

I can't keep up with the number of Spider-Man movies that have been made at this point, but I'll never forget the one I'm referencing. The official title is *Spider-Man 3*, making it even tougher to identify since, nowadays, movies have clever little taglines to distinguish themselves.

Throughout the Spider-Man series, Spider-Man is heartbroken and has vowed vengeance against the man who killed his Uncle Ben.

His Uncle Ben was the man who raised him and his role model. Spider-Man often blames himself because his uncle was waiting to pick him up, and Spider-Man let the robber who shot his uncle go free from the building.

In *Spider-Man 3*, one of the villains in the movie is a force that can latch onto humans and overtake them.

Halfway through the movie, this force latches onto Spider-Man. It becomes clear that this force represents a dark side of human nature and causes Spider-Man to become vengeful.

Spider-Man spends so much time focused on how to get revenge on his uncle's murderer, it stops him from doing what he was called to do—help others!

Chaos ensues around the city as this force has now taken over multiple characters.

Finally, Spider-Man realizes the error in his ways and breaks free from this force that had been holding him captive. In a powerful scene, the chaos finally stops when Spider-Man forgives the man who killed his uncle.

Some of us have a force we've allowed to hold us captive, just like Spider-Man. We are allowing bitterness to root inside of us in the name of "justice."

> We have partnered up with bitterness thinking that it will bring benefit to us.

> We will have justice! We will be vindicated! We will be fought for!

But, my friends, bitterness will only hold you back from pursuing your calling.

It wasn't until Spider-Man woke up and saw what that force was doing to him that he could get back to his calling of fighting evil.

Seeking revenge is a distraction Satan uses to get you away from what God has purposed you to do. The disciples knew this first-hand. In Matthew 10:14, Jesus commanded them, "And if anyone will not receive you or listen to your words, shake off the dust from your feet when you leave that house or town" (ESV).

Later, we see that Paul and Barnabas did just that. In Acts 13, while Paul and Barnabas were traveling and preaching the good news, the Jews stirred up persecution against them. I find it interesting that Acts tells us the Jews used women of high standing and the male leaders of the city. In other words, they used respected indi-viduals to influence people that Paul and Barnabas were wrong in their mission. Sometimes we are in positions where our enemies have the ear of respected individuals or people with great influence.

But Paul and Barnabas's response was exactly as Jesus commanded them—they shook off the dust and went to the next town! They weren't even upset at being thrown out of a city but instead "were filled with joy and with the Holy Spirit" (Acts 13:52 NIV).

The disciples could have wallowed in their hurt; they could have sat around frustrated and wondering where to go next; or they could have hunkered down with discouragement. If they wanted revenge, they could have started a revolution against the high-ranking officials or sought to expose them. But what did they do instead?

They shook off the dust and continued their mission. The Bible says they were filled with joy and the Holy Spirit. They understood what most people don't.

Don't give in to the distraction of seeking revenge over fulfilling your calling.

Revenge Hurts You the Most

The only thing more painful than what someone else did to you is what bitterness will do to you!

We've talked about how bitterness is a root that will take over our hearts and infect all of the other roots in our life if we're not careful.

In my most real moments of mulling over past hurt and pain, I remind myself what bitterness does. I then paint a picture of someone weeding in a garden. Have you ever pulled weeds before?

You must pull them from their root; otherwise, they are at risk of coming back again.

When we first moved into our house, it was the start of spring. We were so focused on moving things in, buying new furniture, and painting that we let all of the yard work go.

We didn't even buy a mower until the end of our first month living in the house (sorry, neighbors!).

Eventually, we looked at the landscaping, and believe it or not, it was hard to tell what was a flower and what was a weed!

Some friends who are good at identifying plants came over to help. Sometimes I would turn to them and say, "We have to do something about this weed." And they would kindly say, "Lauren, that's a flower."

Other plants I'd say, "I can't wait to see what this flower is going to turn into!" And, again, they'd kindly correct me with, "Lauren, that's a weed."

It was hard to tell the difference! Some of the weeds in our back-yard had grown so big you'd need tools to get them out.

Bitterness is the same way. Often, we plant a "revenge plant" right next to our bitterness root in the name of justice and let it grow! Eventually, it takes over and we don't even realize it.

I liken this to a plant known as creeping Charlie. No one is planting this seed, but it springs up in gardens everywhere. It has pretty little flowers and multiplies quickly. It would be easy to tolerate this—it has flowers, after all! But as it multiplies, it restricts other plants' growth and eventually takes over the entire garden. This, too, is an example of when we tolerate bitterness in the name of revenge. At first it seems like the other flowers. It seems harmless at first—maybe even attractive in nature—yet it will take over and kill everything else.

When I recognize that my mind is wandering to places it shouldn't, I close my eyes and picture someone pulling out these weeds in a beautiful garden bed.

I think about how much work it takes to extract a weed that's spread that far and how much power it can take to extract certain deep roots. But I know beyond a shadow of a doubt that the only solution is to pull the weed out with the whole root—otherwise, all our work was in vain.

We're not going to let that stuff back in our heart! We must get it out from the root.

When you are holding on to unforgiveness in the name of revenge, you are only hurting yourself. You are only allowing your heart to be affected.

I love the quote by Lewis B. Smedes in his book *The Art of Forgiving*: "When we forgive, we set a prisoner free and discover that the prisoner we set free is us."[1]

If you are waiting on revenge until you can forgive, I'm afraid the gratification will never come. Even if you are able to get back at someone, will it ever stop there? If Spider-Man were to kill the uncle of the man who killed his uncle, would that have settled the score?

If Paul and Barnabas were to focus on the people who cast them out of Antioch, would they have accomplished what God had graced their life to do?

I remember struggling with hurt from a friend in college. I wanted revenge so badly. But if I'm honest, the justice I felt I was due was much bigger than what they did to me.

It was as if they had committed a minor traffic violation, and I wanted God to sentence them for first-degree murder.

Often, our idea of vengeance is much harsher than what is deserved. This further proves the point that we are slaves to bitterness until we free ourselves by way of forgiveness.

You have bigger things for your life than revenge. You have bigger things to accomplish than getting even. Your life is worth too much to give way to bitterness.

When the world calls us to revenge, God calls us to release. When we release, as unfair a gift as it may seem to give our perpetrator, we are able to move forward in our calling.

We are not being unjust in letting our perpetrator go free without punishment; we are being unjust in holding ourselves hostage until the score is even. We rob ourselves of the purpose God gave to us. We cheat God of all we could accomplish.

No one knew this more than Jesus.

Releasing Is the Ticket to Restoration

When I think about someone who was wronged unfairly, no one was wronged more than Jesus. He lived a perfect life, only to die a criminal's death. But Jesus knew the value of releasing over getting revenge.

That's what was so powerful about Jesus on the cross. He endured suffering beyond what we can imagine for committing no wrong. Yet, some of his last words were: "Father, forgive them, for they know not what they do" (Luke 23:34 ESV).

We see the same attitude of Stephen, the first martyr for the cause of Christ.

> "Lord Jesus, receive my spirit." And falling to his knees
> he cried out with a loud voice, "Lord, do not hold this
> sin against them." And when he had said this, he fell
> asleep. (Acts 7:59–60 ESV)

It's crazy to think that both Jesus and Stephen were advocating for the people who were taking their lives from them as part of their dying request. But they understood something that I often forget.

Giving mercy gives you life. Seeking revenge takes your life away.

When Jesus came, He modeled what the best response should be when he said:

> You have heard that it was said, "An eye for an eye and a
> tooth for a tooth." But I say to you, Do not resist the one
> who is evil. But if anyone slaps you on the right cheek,
> turn to him the other also. And if anyone would sue
> you and take your tunic, let him have your cloak as well.
> And if anyone forces you to go one mile, go with him
> two miles. (Matt. 5:38–41 ESV)

What does this mean? Does this mean that if someone is physically hurting you that you should just stand there and take it? No, that is not what Jesus says.

Rather, Jesus is encouraging you to live in a state of humility to the point that you are unoffendable.

Jesus is telling you to do the opposite of what human nature tells us to do when someone wrongs us. He is leaning into the teaching of the Proverbs:

> If your enemy is hungry, give him bread to eat, and if
> he is thirsty, give him water to drink, for you will heap

> burning coals on his head, and the LORD will reward
> you. (Prov. 25:21–22 ESV)

If you thought heaping burning coals on your enemy's head was the Bible giving you permission to hurt someone, that's not what this verse means.

I used to quote this verse all the time, thinking, *Just by being nice, I'm hurting them.*

Context is very important with this verse. Back in Bible times, people used burning coals as a way to keep warm. This would be the equivalent to giving your enemy your hand warmers at a below-freezing football game.

You're serving them in a kind way—a way that they likely don't deserve.

That's how it works. Repaying violence for violence feels like justice but it does not bring about justice.

The same can be true in any circumstance. Repaying pain for pain. Repaying gossip by spreading rumors about someone. It feels good in the moment, but it is a temporary victory.

It feels like justice.

But Jesus tells us that getting justice for ourselves isn't the way to win.

Rather, when you respond in kindness, your enemy is caught off guard. It typically draws attention to the error in their ways. Even if they have too much shame to correct their error or accept your kindness, they can't help but notice it.

This proverb is saying that when you repay pain for kindness, your enemy notices and God will reward you.

I'll take that route rather than bringing about my own justice any day.

Releasing is the only way. We don't get to decide what justice looks like or when it happens. But that doesn't mean it doesn't happen. You get to release that to God.

We want justice to last forever. We want God to be fighting for us forever for the hurt they caused us. For some, it was the type of hurt that deeply impacted their life. But it doesn't have to be for us to get caught in the bitterness cycle.

Nothing depicts this better than the parable of the unforgiving debtor in Matthew 18:23–35. Jesus describes the kingdom of heaven by using the example of a king who, essentially, wanted to be repaid by all of the servants he lent money to.

One of his debtors owed him ten thousand talents. We know that one talent, a Greek monetary unit in that time, was worth around sixteen years' wages for the average worker. If you contrast that with a standard day's wage today, ten thousand talents would be over a billion dollars.[2] It's an amount so large, there would be no paying it back. The king declared that he should be sold with his wife, children, and everything he owned to pay back his debt.

The debtor began to beg his master to be patient with him and said he would pay it all back in time. The Bible tells us that the king's heart welled up with pity for him and that the king let the debtor go free. He then forgave his debt!

This is clearly symbolic of the debt Jesus paid for us on the cross. It wouldn't have mattered if he worked his whole life, came upon a wealthy inheritance, or won the lottery—the amount was too great, and the king knew this as he forgave his debts. In the same way, when we consider what King Jesus did for us, we should be overwhelmed by the same extravagant forgiveness.

We find out in the next verse that the debtor left the king's presence and went to a man who owed him a few thousand dollars in today's wages. The Bible says he grabbed him by the throat as he demanded he pay it back. The man who owed the debtor a few thousand dollars fell and begged for more time. He, too, asked for patience and said he would pay it all back.

But our original debtor would not show mercy to his debtor. Instead, he had this man thrown into prison because he couldn't pay him back.

The king heard about this and called in the man whose debt he had forgiven. He rebuked him for not showing mercy to his fellow servant after he had just been given mercy for a debt much greater. The king sent the man to be tortured until he had repaid his entire debt. Jesus concludes the parable by saying God will do the same for us if we refuse to forgive one another.

Whenever I hear this story, the contrast between the billion dollars and the thousands of dollars is not lost on me. I always liken it to someone owing a million dollars to the king and their fellow servant owed them pennies. But the reality is, a few thousand dollars is still a lot of money!

Jesus wasn't saying that the man was not owed a lot of money from his fellow servant. Similarly, I'm not suggesting what you are working to forgive is a simple thing to dismiss. Instead, Jesus uses contrasting amounts to depict his point.

The king gave mercy. The debtor was awarded mercy yet sought revenge, which led to him losing his life.

What is revenge worth to you? Is it worth losing your life?

If you ask people who want revenge for something, they certainly have a good reason for it. Their story adds up. They may have been wronged beyond what you can fathom. It's not that it doesn't make sense to want justice by way of revenge. As I shared earlier, the desire for justice is a God characteristic. There isn't anything wrong with wanting justice—the issue is when we take matters into our own hands.

Just like the man who pursued the thousands that were owed to him. It's not that he wasn't owed that money. It's that he overlooked the mercy that had been given to him.

We have been given the gift of eternal life. Despite all our wrong-doing, mercy has been extended to us. Let us not overlook the mercy we have been given because we are seeking revenge on someone else.

The reward for mercy toward others is life everlasting. Yet, the reward for seeking revenge is the sacrifice of your own happiness and calling.

APPLICATION

What does my version of justice look like?

How can I release my idea of justice to God, the Judge?

What is at stake if I don't release this to God?

Prayer: *Lord, you see where I'm at. I'm struggling to release this pain. Even if you restore all they've taken, I am still dealing with the hurt they caused. Help me to keep my eyes focused on releasing instead of revenge. May I stay focused on the mission and the call that you've placed on my life. May I run the race with perseverance and extract any root of bitterness that's holding me back. In Jesus's name, amen!*

NOTES

[1] Lewis B. Smedes, *The Art of Forgiving: When You Need to Forgive and Don't Know How* (New York: Random House, 1997), 178.

[2] "How much is ten thousand talents and a hundred denarii in the parable of Matthew 18 worth according to today's monetary standards?," Words of the Bible, accessed November 20, 2023, https://watv.org/bible_word/monetary-standards/.

ELEVEN

"I Would NEVER Do to Them What They Did to Me"

Ah, we've finally arrived. We're at the point that is going to be the hardest, but most important, to read. The above chapter title was the thought I had echoing in my mind over and over again as I wrestled with the hurt I experienced.

I can't believe they did that.

I would never do something like that.

What did I do to deserve this?

I treat people so much better than how they treated me.

Several years ago, we had Pastor Bryan Jarrett of Northplace Church in Sachse, Texas, come and speak in one of our chapels at the school I attended. He shared a story that changed my life forever.

It was about his friend he went to seminary with. Seminary is basically Bible grad school, and it's for people who are *really* God's favorites. Just kidding. I haven't been to seminary, so if you haven't either, you're in good company. But it is full of people who are devoted to learning and growing in God's Word.

A few years after they had gone to school together, he found out that his friend had shot and killed several people, including children, and later committed suicide himself.

The news article was full of comments from people who had known his friend. They said things like:

> "I can't believe this. He lived down the street from me."

> "I don't understand. We grew up on the same soccer team."

None of these reactions were wrong in nature.

But the theme Pastor Bryan pointed out to us was that people were shocked because they had seen him as someone who was like them—not someone who was a murderer. Seeing as how they found themselves sharing similarities with this individual, they never would have imagined him to be a murderer since they could never imagine themselves committing murder. In other words, he shared that their thoughts were: *he must not have been as similar to me as I thought because I would never do what he did.*

It was then that Pastor Bryan shared a quote that rocked my entire view of Christianity. He said:

"You can't understand the good news of salvation until you understand the depravity of your own sin."

Let's pause for a minute.

I couldn't believe what he was suggesting. *Is he suggesting that I'm just as much a sinner as that man? He must be crazy! That's ridiculous, not to mention offensive!*

But I listened as he unpacked the reality of the gospel message, and by the end, I had come to terms with what he was saying. It forever changed the way I see salvation.

The same sin that was in this man who murdered others was the same sin that existed in me. It may not have been as out of control, or maybe it didn't act out in that way. But whichever way you slice it, that sin lived inside of me too.

I'm not about to accuse you of any crime. I'm not about to tell you that it's only a matter of time before you commit a terrible crime.

What I'm going to tell you is the three words that helped me enough to find healing:

I'm

no

better.

To really understand this truth and how it relates to bitterness, we need to go all the way back to the origin of sin.

Sin in the Beginning

In Genesis, we're told that God first created the heavens and the earth, the birds, animals, and, ultimately, man. The first man was Adam, and the first woman was Eve.

God gave them ownership and the ability to do all but one thing: they must not eat the fruit from the tree of the knowledge of good and evil.

I don't know about you, but I always saw that tree's name as a mouthful. It took me a long time to recognize what it meant and symbolized. What this tree did was open your eyes to the good and evil in the world.

You know when people ask the question, "Why do bad things happen to good people?"

While I don't dissect that question in this book, I can tell you it's only because we have the knowledge of good and evil that we can even discern what is right and what is wrong.

In Genesis 3:1, the devil had been cast out of heaven and, in the form of a snake, went up to Eve, leading with this line: "Did God really say, 'You must not eat from any tree in the garden'?" (NIV).

He convinced her to eat from the tree of knowledge of good and evil. She turned around and convinced her husband, Adam, to eat from this tree as well. After God found out that Adam and Eve ate from this tree, he put a curse on the snake, man, and woman.

He then said, as is recorded in Genesis 3:22: "The man has now become like one of us, knowing good and evil. He must not be allowed to reach out his hand and take also from the tree of life and eat, and live forever" (NIV).

Did you catch that? The tree of life was what they were eating from, and that allowed them to live forever. It was a real-life fountain of youth!

But man chose to disobey God, which is what caused our sinful nature.

This is why we would say that, for the sake of argument, even a baby who has not lived long enough to have sinned has adopted a sinful nature just by being a part of humankind.

"The man has now become like one of us, knowing good and evil."

It's not necessarily contingent upon who you are or what you've done—it's the species you're a part of.

When Adam and Eve ate the apple, it symbolized mankind deciding between good and evil with their own wisdom. This wasn't God's wisdom. It was the wisdom of people who were created by God, the people who trusted a talking snake and jumped at the first chance to disobey God, the same people who didn't do much of anything other than chill in a garden prior to eating from the forbidden tree.

I've chilled in a garden before. Olive Garden. It was great until they stopped bringing the free breadsticks. Before we continue, I want to thank you for still being here despite my terrible jokes!

When they ate the apple, it wasn't necessarily this paralyzing moment when, all of a sudden, the earth started shaking and Adam and Eve broke all ten of what would become the Ten Commandments simultaneously.

No, rather, it meant that humanity was going to decide good and evil for themselves using their wisdom. And they didn't have a lot of it. The suggestion that they could do this without failing was an unattainable goal.

What is most interesting about this is that their inability to determine good and evil is part of what got them here in the first place.

There are two things about this scripture that have perplexed me. Have you ever wondered why Eve was drawn to the talking snake? I don't know many people drawn to snakes.

I don't know about you, but the only influence snakes have over me is to take the long way around if one of them is on the sidewalk.

The second thing I always found perplexing was that the snake was cursed to "crawl on [its] belly and . . . eat dust all the days of [its] life" (Gen. 3:14 NIV). I could never picture a snake walking up to me on two legs. Even four legs seemed like a stretch.

I would suggest it's because snakes used to have wings. In Isaiah 6, Isaiah describes a vision he has of the throne room of the Lord. In it, he describes the creatures and angels that surround the Lord. In this passage, he uses the Hebrew word *sarap*, which refers to a serpent every other time it's mentioned in the Old Testament.[1]

Likely to show the distinction, in this instance, it is translated as "seraphim" and is commonly known as a general name of angels along with *cherubim*. When scholars draw what they believe a seraphim looked like, it is essentially a snake with wings.

This would explain why the snake was cursed to the ground. It did not walk; it flew. It also explains why Eve was drawn to the snake. It looked ever-so-similar to a heavenly being.

This further validates the point that man is going to fail at distinguishing between good and evil. Eve was not deceived by a being presenting as the complete opposite of God. Rather, Eve was deceived by a being mimicking God, and she, being human, could not tell the difference.

This inability to distinguish correctly was a sin, and it made them susceptible to sin or, in Hebrew, *khata*.

Khata is the word used most in the Old Testament for sin, and it means to fail or miss the goal.

It's indicative of humans failing God and each other by their own actions, which are driven by human wisdom rather than God's wisdom.

And how does our human wisdom advise us to live? Psychologists will tell you that at the core of every human is an inclination to take care of themselves first. It's driven by selfish tendencies, not the wisdom of the gospel, which is to put others above yourself.

That's why when God gave the Ten Commandments, five of them were laws for how to honor him, and five of them were laws for how to honor others.

Those laws give us our best examples of what sin, or missing the mark, can look like, because, by nature, we don't adhere to God's wisdom. Instead, we adhere to our own, thanks to the incident in Genesis 3.

The Bible also indicates that God doesn't compartmentalize sin. Sin is sin.

Murder is sin. Lying is sin. Gossip is sin. Wanting what your neighbor has is sin. Looking at someone with lust who isn't your spouse is sin. Treating someone as less than a child of God is sin.

It's all bad news. It all misses the mark. It's not ranked as "worse or better than what they did."

It's sin. It's what keeps us from being aligned with God's wisdom, and it's what kept us from eating from the tree of life and living forever.

To reframe Romans 6:23, it's not just that "the wages of sin is death" (NIV). It's also that our desire to decide for ourselves what is good and what is evil eliminated our opportunity to live forever.

But aren't you thankful there's a "but"?

But the gift of God is eternal life! God gives good gifts!

That's why he sent his son Jesus to pave a way for us.

I like the way the New Living Translation says it in 1 Peter 2:22–24:

> He never sinned, nor ever deceived anyone. He did not
> retaliate when he was insulted, nor threaten revenge
> when he suffered. He left his case in the hands of God,
> who always judges fairly. He personally carried our sins
> in his body on the cross so that we can be dead to sin
> and live for what is right. By his wounds you are healed.

Jesus came and lived by God's wisdom in doing right to others and to God. He let God fight his battles. He never sinned. But he carried our sins in his human body to the cross so that we might die to our sin and have eternal life.

What a powerful truth!

How Is That Fair?

I was talking to a friend the other day, and she was expressing frustration with the gospel.

In particular, the story below gave her pause.

In Luke 23, we find Jesus nailed to a cross with a criminal on his right and a criminal on his left. One of the criminals beside him began mocking Jesus. The other criminal stood up for Jesus, saying, "We deserve to die for our crimes, but this man hasn't done anything wrong" (Luke 23:41 NLT). He then asked Jesus to remember him when Jesus entered his kingdom. Jesus, full of mercy and grace, told the man he would be with him in paradise when he died.

My friend's frustration was with the fact that the criminal lived a shameful life and, in the last minutes of his life, he got accepted into God's kingdom.

"It's just not fair," she claimed. "He got to just run around and do whatever he wanted his whole life, and he still got in?"

Many of us may say we are excited to offer grace to the imprisoned murderer who gives his life to Jesus while incarcerated. But my friend's aforementioned thought becomes more relatable when we think about celebrities whose lives don't appear to align with God's Word, yet they have "God first" in their social media bio.

Is it fair that those people still get into heaven? They get to indulge in their sinful desires and, by accepting Jesus, God will still forgive them in the final hour?

Friend, that is the beauty of the gospel! If no other message, that's the message.

If we mess up our entire lives, we can have redemption by the blood of Jesus. It was never about what we did right anyway. It was always about Jesus!

Of course, this may lead one to think they should live as they want to and turn to Christ in the final hour. Paul addresses this in Romans 6 when he reminds us that we have died to sin so we must not live in it any longer. In verse 6 he reminds us that "we are no longer slaves to sin" (NLT).

Without pivoting from the original message, I want to remind you that the people who live their lives as they want do not have more fulfilling lives. They are slaves to these desires. Following God's Word is the manual by which one can have a happy, fulfilled, and content life.

Regardless of how someone lives their life, we are assured redemption is possible even in their final moments. If you're struggling with this like I did, I would challenge you with this question: How much of one's life must be lived in righteousness to get into heaven?

Is it over half? Is it 40 percent?

Is it trying to be a good person from a young age?

Is it accepting Jesus in your heart early on and then messing up 30 percent of the time but feeling really bad about it?

What are the metrics by which you feel someone is worthy of the redemptive power of Jesus Christ?

To define it at all is to get in our own way. It misses the point. Jesus Christ died for you and for me so that we may have eternal life!

I'm

no

better.

"But They Really Need Jesus"

You may still be thinking something like: *I'm no better? Of course I'm better than them! They're immature. They're ruthless. They don't have a heart! They are living a sinful lifestyle!*

Honestly, all those things may be true.

The person who wronged you may be immature. They may have some growing to do. They may have been selfish. They may be living a sinful lifestyle. They may even have personality disorders or personality types that are manipulative, controlling, or prideful.

I'm not suggesting the other person doesn't have things to work on. It's likely you have grown in areas they still need to grow in.

What I am telling you is that the cross levels the playing field. We will not successfully move forward in freedom until we grasp this truth. The Bible says in Romans 6:23 that "the wages of sin is death, but the gift of God is eternal life" (NIV).

We get so caught up in our pride. We get so caught up in the idea that someone could possibly sin against us when we sin against others as well!

I'm not trying to minimize what they did. I hope you never hurt someone the way they hurt you! And I pray you are never hurt again the way they hurt you this time!

But it doesn't change the fact that to be human is to need a savior. There isn't a ranking system of how much one needs a savior.

There is no such thing as categories with people who kind of need Jesus and who *really* need Jesus.

> "You can't understand the good news of salvation until you
> understand the depravity of your own sin."
> —Pastor Bryan Jarrett

This will be the hardest thing to come to terms with, but if you can grasp it, you can find freedom from anything someone does to you.

That's why forgiveness takes humility. It takes recognizing that we're not better. It takes recognizing that we're just as much in need of saving even if our sin looks different from someone else's.

I love the way C. S. Lewis puts it: "To be a Christian means to forgive the inexcusable because God has forgiven the inexcusable in you."[2]

You may not do to them what they would do to you, but forgiveness requires the humility to see that you have both sinned against God and are both worthy of his judgment.

I remember when I was going through my hard season, I finally was able to say, "I may not have done the same things that they did to me. I may be disappointed, frustrated, or hurt by their actions. But I can accept that I am just as in need of a savior. And, in that way, my adversary and I are in the same boat." By repeating thoughts like this, we can turn our hatred into gratitude for what God did for us.

When you accept your own flaws enough to give grace to others with flaws, you open the door to a freedom unlike anything you've ever experienced.

Believing that you would never do anything as bad as your offender is the lie used to justify unforgiveness. It's time to put our human wisdom aside and align with God's wisdom.

We will not give in to the lie any longer that we are so much better than the people who wronged us. It is a lie that only leads to pride, and as such, it exacerbates our pain even more.

Thank you, Jesus, for the gift of eternal life for me and for my adversary.

APPLICATION

In case you need some time to grapple with the above, here are some practical things you can do to help:

- Meditate on the gospel during your prayer time (Matthew, Mark, Luke, or John).

- Have an at-home service in which you take communion, read the gospel, and position your heart to remember what Jesus did for us.
- Read Isaiah 53, where it talks about what Jesus would endure for us.
- Read and reflect on Leviticus, when the Israelites had to atone for their sins without Jesus.

Prayer: *Dear God, I humble myself before you. I recognize that I am a sinner who needs your grace and mercy. I thank you for dying for my sins so I can be with you. I know that no matter how many times I fail you, you forgive me until completion. Please help me to do the same with others.*

NOTES

[1]"H8314 - śārāp̄ - Strong's Hebrew Lexicon (KJV)," Blue Letter Bible, accessed November 28, 2023, https://www.blueletterbible.org/lexicon/h8314/kjv/wlc/0-1/.
[2]C. S. Lewis, *The Weight of Glory and Other Addresses* (1941; reis., New York: Macmillan, 1980), 125.

TWELVE

"I Didn't Think CHRISTIANS Would Do This"

Whether you're a DC fan or a Marvel fan (or both), superhero movies are some of the most popular in the United States. Marvel and DC movies have accounted for almost 25 percent of the top one hundred highest-grossing box office films of all time.[1]

There's something people love about a superhero defeating a villain and saving innocent lives.

I think part of why we love these movies is because they have expected endings. There may be things along the way that surprised you, but in every movie, you can expect the villain to be against the superhero and the superhero to ultimately conquer the villain.

After all, no one is shocked when the villain in a superhero movie tries to kill the superhero—that's how they developed the plot in the first place.

Imagine the shock if a superhero were to wrong someone and become villainous. If a superhero ever turned evil, we as the audience wouldn't be settled until that superhero had been redeemed to fight for good again.

Sometimes that's how it feels when a Christian is the one who hurts us.

The most painful seasons of my life have involved hurt from other Christians.

It's one thing to be hurt by someone who doesn't know Christ. Similar to the traditional superhero plot, you almost expect it. You can excuse that hurt with thoughts like this:

They may not know any better.

That's human nature.

I can't expect them to live by biblical principles when they haven't made the Bible the authority over their life.

It's not necessarily easier to move on from, but it can be easier to understand.

However, some of us have had the superhero script flipped on us. It's felt like the people we should have trusted acted as or became the villain in our stories. Some of us reading this book were hurt growing up by Christians. Maybe mentors, Sunday school teachers, or parents had the best intentions but projected their insecurities or flaws onto us.

Maybe you vividly remember a Sunday school teacher or a youth leader sharing a skewed depiction of God—not because they meant to, but because they themselves were still learning who God really is, as we will continue to do for our entire lives.

Perhaps you were hurt by a godly individual you were dating. I'll tell you right now, if they used the old "God told me we weren't supposed to be together" line, it's probably for the best that it didn't work out.

It could be that you were hurt by someone who told you they acted the way they did because God told them to.

Many of us have experienced church hurt, either when we were younger or when we grew up.

It's understandable when you remember that the church is run by imperfect people, but that doesn't make it any easier to hear someone stand on a platform and interpret God's Word if they're the one who hurt you.

My chief thoughts when I had been hurt by another Christian were these:

- *I feel naïve for trusting you and now I don't know if I can trust again.*
- *I thought we were on the same team.*
- *I don't understand why God still loves them when they've hurt me. I want God to be on my side.*

None of these thoughts make us anything other than human. I'm no longer ashamed of feeling this way—it's how I felt! We're going to validate our feelings and our thoughts to heal, remember?

While these thoughts may not be bad, mulling over them is sure to lead to bitterness.

Bitterness will destroy your life. The Bible is clear about that.

Unfortunately, when you have bitterness toward other Christians, Satan uses it to accelerate the destruction bitterness brings.

Satan is an opportunist. He sees an opportunity to take the bitter root that was already deepening in your heart and use it to turn you against God, the church, and anything to do with religion.

I don't know about you guys, but I grew up singing the song:

> Higher, higher, higher, higher, higher, higher, higher, higher, lift Jesus higher, higher.

> Lower, lower, lower, lower, lower, lower, lower, lower, stomp Satan lower, lower.[2]

And the song:

> He's under my feet, he's under my feet, he's under my feet, he's under my feet, Satan is under my feet![3]

Ah, the nineties were a repetitive time.

Those songs were a great combination of fun and power, but sometimes, I think they led to me thinking all I'd have to do was just send Satan lower. I thought all I had to do was whisper, "Leave, please," and that would take care of it.

In other words, I think because we know that God is more powerful, we forget that Satan is powerful, too. The Bible never insinuates that Satan is weak.

Satan would love for you to think he's weak, but he is a powerful being that has waged war on the thing his enemy, God, loves most: us. Bitterness is one of his favorite tools, and there is not a type of bitterness he loves more than bitterness toward the thing he hates most: God.

What should our attitude be? How do we handle our emotions when other Christians hurt us? I'm glad you asked!

Follow the Biblical Model

Did you know there is a biblical model for handling hurt by another Christian? Jesus breaks it down for us in a way that's easier to understand than your IKEA furniture assembly manual, yet many are unaware of it. My prayer in highlighting this is that more Christians take the biblical model for handling hurt seriously.

The Bible is clear.

Matthew 18 tells us there are steps to addressing hurt. First, you take it to that person in private and discuss it with them. This feels so intimidating, yet it's how we would want someone to address it if we committed the offense. Second, you can address it with the person and one or two others to have your words confirmed and for people to hold you accountable. Last, if they still won't listen, take it to the church. In today's world, I see this as church leadership, your small group leader, or the leader of the area you serve in. This third step is so someone in biblical authority over them can address the behavior.

In summary:

1. Go to the person privately.
2. Bring another person.
3. Take it to the church.

I don't know about you, but I can think of a lot of times when I've gotten those backward. I might not have announced it on our church social media, but I took it to the body of the church—my friends in the church—before even mentioning it to the person who I felt wronged me.

Too often, we go to others in the name of "getting mentorship," "seeking wisdom," or, the biggest offender, "asking for prayer for a situation."

Perhaps we lack the maturity to know how to approach a situation. That's okay, as it can be intimidating at first. In those circumstances, I'd encourage you to go to one person whom you trust if you must. But more people need to know that the Bible doesn't include that in its model.

The Bible says to go to the person privately and point out the offense. It also says that if you do this in the right way, there's a good chance you'll win them over.

When I first started in my career, I remember being hurt by a coworker of mine. This was someone I trusted, and we found ourselves in a social setting together when I felt like I was made fun of. While he wasn't responsible for the original comments, he expanded on them and laughed with everyone.

It may not be fair, but I found myself more upset with him than the people who made the comments in the first place. I felt that he gave people permission to mock me, and I expected more from him as my friend.

I wanted to go to another friend who works with us and "talk through it." But instead, I followed the biblical model. When I went to him, I led with this: "I want to express something to you, and I want you to know that I'm only sharing this with you because I have too much respect for you to share it with other people."

One of the biggest things that causes people to jump to defend themselves is the feeling that you've shared this with other people first and have tarnished their reputation.

I expressed how I valued our friendship and that I had been hurt by his actions. I asked that, going forward, he not condone others' actions when they're making fun of me.

The conversation went well. He understood where I was coming from and thanked me for going to him first. He even made the comment that, because I went to him first, it strengthened the trust between us going forward.

Of course, some may make the case that I was being overly sensitive or shouldn't have bothered him with it in the first place, but here's the deal: I knew that to get over this, I was going to talk about it! I decided to give the biblical model a try first so as not to let my words create more damage.

In Mark 11:24–25 (NLT), Jesus tells us:

> I tell you, you can pray for anything, and if you believe that you've received it, it will be yours. But when you are praying, first forgive anyone you are holding a grudge against, so that your Father in heaven will forgive your sins, too.

I heard a story from a missionary once who told about people entering a worship service only to get up and leave to go talk to the people whom they were holding a grudge against before they resumed their worship.

That's how seriously they took the verse.

While we may not put this into practice during our church services, I think this verse speaks to the integrity that we must have to approach God's throne. God desires that we have clean hands and a pure heart as we approach him with our prayers.

It's interesting that he doesn't say, "But when you are praying, it's important that you're honest with God about all the sin you've committed; otherwise, God won't respond to your prayers."

The Bible does talk about confessing our sins, but Jesus told us the priority for entering his presence with a pure heart is forgiveness. It's that important.

When we follow the biblical model, we don't just live at peace with others; it enhances our prayer life!

You may be asking the question: *Yes, but do I have to go to them in every situation?* The short answer is that I don't believe you do have to address every wrong with each person.

If I had to address each time I felt offended with the person who offended me, I'd have my own drama television show by now. Sometimes it's better to release it with God's help than to address it. But the purity of your heart is what's most important as you enter God's presence.

How can we position our hearts to be pure and holy before God? I have two themes below to help us as we move forward!

Have an Attitude like Paul's

One of the great difficulties of being hurt by another believer is seeing God go on to use that person for his kingdom. You may be confused or angry that he would work in their life after what they did to you. In this situation, we can learn from the astounding response of Paul.

If you're familiar with the Bible, when I say the name "Paul," a lot of things may come to mind. Champion of the faith. Formerly the enemy of Christians. Wrote half of the New Testament.

Paul was like the poster child for preaching the gospel. He set the standard and walked closely with the Lord in a way that should make us jealous. He preached the gospel every chance he got. The way he wrote most of the New Testament was by way of writing letters to other churches, either to convict or encourage them in godliness.

There was just one problem: he made those in authority mad.

Paul found himself in prison on a number of occasions. He's still known for his great attitude despite it all.

In Philippians 1:15–18, we find Paul imprisoned in what most scholars agree was Rome, although there is debate about this. If Paul was imprisoned in Rome, he was imprisoned in the city where he always felt called to preach. It was his dream to preach the gospel to the masses, and Rome was the best place to do this.

While he was in prison, he heard of other preachers spreading lies about him.

It's unclear what they were saying, but it is clear that they were trying to get people to turn against Paul. Out of speculation, they may have been saying things like:

> *Paul is in prison because God is mad at him.*

> *Paul is in prison because he has some kind of hidden sin in his life.*

> *If God wanted Paul to be out of prison, he'd get him out of prison, but God is punishing Paul.*

No doubt they used Paul's past against him, as that was an easy target.

You may be thinking, *Those guys don't sound like they were Christian preachers.*

But they were! Paul says they were. He didn't claim they were preaching false doctrine or say that people should ignore them—quite the opposite!

His response brings me to my knees! Paul addressed that some who were preaching Christ wanted the spotlight. They were excited that Paul was in prison, and they would prefer that he stay there so they could be the ultimate voice among believers. The other group had pure hearts and motives. They wanted to help Paul because they saw him as their teammate in sharing the good news.

Paul concluded this passage by declaring that whether someone's motives are pure or not, the only thing that matters is that Christ is preached. He explained that as long as it's someone who's preaching Christ, what does it matter if they have good motives or bad motives?

I can't believe it. Other Christians were jeering at Paul!

If I had been Paul, I would have written down their names, phone numbers, and addresses in my next letter so my crew could pay them a visit.

I would have gone to God and asked him to strike them down like lightning. *I'm spending all of my time and energy on worrying about which of my friends is going to be my friend when I get out. I may even listen to some of the lies they're sharing and worry that they might be right! I thought we were on the same team, and they aren't being good teammates!*

Instead, Paul says he's going to cheer them on?

Paul says he's on their side?

Paul says he's happy that Christ is being preached?

How often do we get more caught up in the person delivering the message than the message that's being delivered?

Believe me, I've been there!

> We want to make sure the pastor's heart is in the right place before we'll accept a word from them.
>
> We want to be challenged by God's Word, but only by a person we deem worthy of challenging us.

When we hear of someone's wrongdoing, there's something inside of us that says, *Finally, I can take my seat as a judge.*

But Paul, the victim in this scenario, was cheering them on!

But he was not just cheering them on to preach the gospel. For some of them, he was cheering them on to accomplish his dream of preaching the gospel in Rome.

That was Paul's dream.

Let that sink in.

Paul was cheering on those who had wronged him to live out his very dream.

How many times do we look at God and complain when we think the person who got what we wanted isn't deserving of it?

I'll be the first to admit I have not grown to that level of maturity. But I have concluded that this is the standard I want for my life.

> *That church that has said a lot of bad things about our church saw fifty people get saved on Sunday? Fantastic! Fifty people got saved!*

> *The pastor who wronged me just got more followers for posting reels about Jesus? How cool is it that God can use anyone to minister?*

> *The person who tried to ruin my life is being used at their church now? Praise God!*

These aren't my first responses. But I'm committed to reframing all of my human responses into the attitude of Paul.

Colossians 3:2 tells us, "Set your minds on things above, not on earthly things" (NIV).

When you set your heart on the eternal, you gain perspective. In light of eternity, little matters other than the message of the gospel.

It was with this mindset that Paul was able to say, "What does it matter?" (Phil. 1:18 NIV).

> *What does it matter if people are talking bad about me?*

> *What does it matter if people think God's mad at me?*

His focus was on what God thought and the mission he had set out for him.

Have an Attitude like the Christians Martyred by Paul

Like those whom Paul martyred, we need to keep an eternal perspective.

I remember in 2020 I declared my word for the year was *eternity*. I didn't want to dwell on things that didn't matter in heaven, I remember telling a group of friends and my mentors at their New Year's Eve party.

Little did I know, that year, I would be planning a wedding during a pandemic!

I mean, with an eternity perspective, it's not that big of a deal that we couldn't host everyone we wanted to on our special day, but in the moment it was!

Sometimes it's hard to let go of things in the moment. It's okay to recognize that the here and now is easier to focus on than eternity.

But some people weren't given that luxury.

I'm talking about the people who were persecuted by Paul, or Saul, rather. The same Paul we just talked about above who was a hero of the faith went by the name Saul for most of his life. It's kind of like when your best friend growing up decides to go by James at his corporate job instead of Jimmy. You understand, but it can be hard to retrain your brain. For those unfamiliar with Paul's story, I'd encourage you to read Acts 7–9.

The short version is this:

In Acts 8:1, we're told that Saul was one of the witnesses who completely agreed with the killing of Stephen. Stephen was the first Christian to be martyred for their faith, and some could argue this was at the hand of Saul.

In Acts 9, we're told that Saul convinced the high priest to allow him to arrest both men and women. The Bible says that Saul "was uttering threats with every breath and was eager to kill the Lord's followers" (Acts 9:1 NLT).

Then, God got ahold of him. He appeared to Saul and completely changed his life. Saul did a 180! He began to be called Paul after his complete transformation in Christ.

We often hear that story and think, *Wow, isn't God good? He turned Paul's life around and used him! God can use anyone!* We forget about the people like Stephen, who died at Paul's prompting.

We forget about the people who were beaten and thrown into prison and persecuted because of Paul. The villain became the superhero. Talk about a plot twist.

It doesn't occur to us what they thought of God using someone like Paul to be famous throughout the world. There will be people whose names we never know that were beaten by Paul just for being Christians. However, Paul is the one who is famous.

If I'm them, I'm saying, *God? This guy? You could've chosen anyone! It didn't have to be me. I mean, I think it'd be great if you chose me, but—this guy?*

I don't understand why you still love him when he hurt me.

One of the hardest parts for me of being hurt by another Christian was seeing God bless their life. Some of the people who hurt me were promoted within the church. It was hard enough to watch them worship and feel that they were genuine! Now they were being honored, too?

But it's not just promotion within ministry positions. Some of the Christians who hurt me got things I wanted. They got married before me. They bought a house before me. It felt like God was blessing them, and I was getting left behind.

It was hard to see my friends be friends with them. I felt like everyone should be on my side. I knew it wasn't a fair ask, but it's how I felt.

Yet, God said, "Go, for Saul is my chosen instrument to take my message to the Gentiles and to kings, as well as to the people of Israel. And I will show him how much he must suffer for my name's sake" (Acts 9:15–16 NLT).

We don't always understand the ways of God. But, compared to eternity, what does it matter so long as heaven is populated?

There were people who greeted Paul in heaven whose lives were cut short because of him. That's a sobering thought. But there were thousands more who entered heaven because God chose to use a man who had hurt other people.

Forgiveness takes perspective.

God, Use Them

My question to you is this: What is it worth to you for God to not use the person who hurt you?

I know your human flesh would feel better. I know it'd boost your ego and make you feel like God is on your side. I know that because I've felt that way, too.

But I'll ask again: What is it worth to you for God to not use the person who hurt you?

> What if he wants to use them to write a book that's going to impact your children some day?

> What if he wants to use them to write a song that's going to bring healing to thousands?

> What if he wants to use them to preach a message where hundreds accept Christ as Savior?

Will you give God permission to use the people who've wronged you?

He doesn't need your permission, but it will help in your healing process. Let's settle it in our hearts that just because God is using someone who hurt us, it doesn't mean he forgot about our pain.

Just because God is using someone, it doesn't mean he "sides with them."

God didn't use Paul because Paul was right when he was persecuting Christians.

> God didn't use Paul as a way to affirm Paul for the actions in his past toward other Christians.

> God used Paul because of who God is, not who Paul was.

Aren't you thankful for that?

I can't promise that the people who wronged you were acting Christlike. I can't tell you that they will change before God will use them.

I can only promise you that God, in his justice, will make things right. For now, our job is to keep an eternal perspective. And one day, perhaps in eternity, we will come to understand why.

APPLICATION

Take a minute to reflect. This was tough to grasp, and we covered a lot of ground.

How does this shift my mindset going forward when hurt by other Christians?

Still struggling? That's normal. Pray something like this: *Lord, you see that I'm struggling with this hurt. I'm struggling that it came from another member of the team, my Christian brother or sister. I pray that you would help heal this hurt in my heart. Help me to be kingdom-minded and see the bigger picture. Help me to move past my pain and see them as you see them. If it be your will, I pray we would both reach people for your kingdom and your glory. In Jesus's name, amen.*

If that prayer was tough to pray, I want you to know this:

When you can pray for your adversary to be used by God, you're standing on the edge of freedom.

NOTES

[1] "Top Lifetime Grosses," Box Office Mojo, accessed November 6, 2023, https://www.boxofficemojo.com/chart/top_lifetime_gross/?area=XWW.

[2] "Higher Higher," featuring Imisi and Avion, track 2 on Christafari, *Reggae Sunday School*, Gotee Records, 2005.

[3] Lindell Cooley, vocalist, "Enemy's Camp," by Richard Smallwood, track 2 on *Revival at Brownsville*, Integrity Music, 1995.

THIRTEEN

"God, Why Did You ALLOW This?"

One of the biggest questions we have when we go through adversity is:

Why?

When I think about all of the people in the Bible we've discussed, I'm sure they had similar questions.

David was probably asking,

- God, why did Saul have to hate me?
- Why did he try to kill me?
- Why couldn't he have just passed away in war and I be brought in as the next king?
- Why did our paths have to cross?

Job, I'm sure, spent many sleepless nights wondering,

- God, where are you?
- Why are you doing this?

- Are you doing this?
- If not, why are you allowing this?
- Was it something I did?
- Are you really all-powerful if you can't stop this?

Shadrach, Meshach, and Abednego were probably thinking,

- God, why did we have to live during this time period?
- Why couldn't you leave this for someone else?
- Why didn't you soften the heart of the king?
- Why didn't you blind them so it looked like we bowed down to the idol?
- Did we have to get all the way to the thrown-into-the-furnace part?

I've seen the question of "why" plague people for years and years.

When I was in school, I went through a very difficult season. I couldn't make sense of the hurt I felt. I couldn't understand why God allowed it. I couldn't grasp how it seemed like God let people get away with it. Furthermore, I didn't understand why it seemed like their lives were being blessed despite their actions.

It flipped my worldview upside down.

For so long I had believed, *If I do this, God will do this*, or something like, *If someone behaves badly, God will smite them.*

Just kidding. But I really did start creating formulas in my head for "if–then" scenarios.

Without realizing it, it formed a lot of the foundation of my theology.

I wasn't trusting in God as much as I was trusting in the formula I had created.

If I do good things, God will be happy with me, and I will get good things.

If I do bad things, God won't be happy with me, and I will self-destruct.

Of course, God's Word tells us that there are principles, like in Galatians 6:7, that "a man reaps what he sows" (NIV).

We can't discount that our actions, both good and bad, have consequences. But what we need to understand is that there is not a perfect formula.

Pretty soon, my faith became contingent upon making sure God honored the formula I had set up for him. When I saw people who had hurt me seemingly getting good gifts from God, it shook me. I had to reevaluate. I had to go back to the drawing board. Something in my equation was wrong.

So I started seeking for answers. I did this by reading the Word of God.

The Bible says that the Word of God is living and active, sharper than any two-edged sword (Heb. 4:12). It's important when you commit to reading God's Word that you also commit to understanding God's Word. Reading God's Word and understanding God's Word are two different things.

Anyone can read God's Word. It takes study and revelation to understand God's Word.

When I had crafted my formula, I was reading the Bible and taking it at face value.

When I developed fundamental truths about God, I was growing in the understanding of God's Word.

(As a sidenote, one of the best ways to do this is to pick up a study Bible. I like the ESV Study Bible, but there are others. I also enjoy watching videos by The Bible Project. They make sense of just about everything!)

The idea of me creating another formula to fit God into didn't seem like a good one, so I found fundamental truths that I could lean on even when I didn't understand. I began writing down these truths and scripture on notecards. I carried those notecards with me wherever I went. They served as my reminder when thoughts crept in.

One of my favorites was Psalm 125:1 (NIV): "Those who trust in the LORD are like Mount Zion, which cannot be shaken but endures forever."

When my formula was crumbling beneath me, I remembered that I am like Mount Zion when I trust in the Lord.

Let's unpack six truths from God's Word that we can know beyond a shadow of a doubt. These will help us whenever we're struggling with something that didn't turn out like we thought it should.

God Is in Control

Going back to Job 38, God is all-knowing, all-powerful, and omnipresent. There is not a thing going on that he does not see, and there is not a person on this earth outside of his love.

"Have you ever given orders to the morning?" (Job 38:12 NIV).

When wrestling with your situation, it's important to know that God is in control.

You aren't just praying to a God who can't do anything about your request.

You are praying to a God who created the heavens and the earth. He gives the orders to the morning. He is the one who tells the winds and the rains where to go.

I find this verse so reassuring:

> He will not let your foot slip—*he who watches over you will not slumber;* indeed, he who watches over Israel will neither slumber nor sleep. The LORD watches over you— the LORD is your shade at your right hand; the sun will not harm you by day, nor the moon by night. *The Lord will keep you from all harm—he will watch over your life;* the LORD will watch over your coming and going both now and forevermore. (Ps. 121:3–8 NIV—emphasis mine)

For a few years before I got married, I lived alone. Without the company of a roommate or a husband to protect me, I had a hard time falling asleep every night. The ice maker would make its routine noises, and I would get scared. These verses brought me great comfort on those nights because they reminded me that the Lord is in control at all hours of the night. It revealed his nature.

He doesn't slumber.

While you sleep, God's awake. He's watching over every detail of your life.

God is in control.

God Loves Us More Than We Can Fathom

My made-up formula said that God loved me unless I did something wrong.

It said that God loved me if I went to church on Wednesday nights, too.

It said that God loved me if I made time to do devotions that day.

If I dropped the ball on any of these things, I shouldn't expect anything from God.

But Romans 8:38–39 (NIV) tells us:

> For I am convinced that neither death nor life, neither angels nor demons, neither the present nor the future, nor any powers, neither height nor depth, *nor anything else in all creation, will be able to separate us from the love of God that is in Christ Jesus our Lord.* (emphasis mine)

Even though we know God loves us, it can be easy to imagine God is mad at us sometimes. After all, we reason, you can love someone and be mad at them.

These verses remind us that no matter what we do, what we've done, and what we're going to do, we can't stop God's love. Just like God isn't sleeping on the job, he doesn't have "off days."

God doesn't have mood swings, nor is he fickle. No, God's very nature assures us that he will continue to love us even when we don't love him back.

2 Timothy 2:13 (NLT) says, "If we are unfaithful, he remains faithful, for he cannot deny who he is."

Aren't you thankful God's love is not contingent upon who we are but rather on who he is?

Whenever I begin to doubt God's love, these words echo in my head, my faith builds, and I remember that I serve the God who is both in control and loves me!

God Is a Good God

Do you ever get a text from someone, and you read it in their angry voice? I've gotten some text messages from people that have sent me over the edge for no reason simply because I assumed their voice inflection.

Studies have told us that our verbal words are only 7 percent of communication. The rest is nonverbal.[1] That means texting has some challenges. This was especially true before emojis were popular.

I remember when I was leading our worship team, my pastor asked me to meet after our prayer service one Saturday. He was just coming back from vacation, and I remember thinking, *If he wants to meet me this urgently, I've done something wrong.*

I didn't get much out of prayer service that day. Afterward, we met at a nearby coffee shop. I remember shaking a little.

He smiled and asked, "How's it going?"

I opened up about how hard I was working, and I shared all of my flaws and things I needed to work on, thinking I could beat him to whatever he wanted to talk about.

Finally, after I covered everything I could think of, I just came out with the question: "Are those some of the things you wanted to meet about?"

He smiled and said, "No, I just wanted to see how you were doing, but I'm happy to talk through those if you need my help on any of them."

"Really?" I asked, getting emotional. "That's it?"

"Yeah. That's it. We just haven't met in a while, and I just wanted to see how things were going."

I broke down. "I thought you were going to fire me."

I was a volunteer.

Looking back at the situation, I see how much I had worked things up in my head.

This wasn't even after a history of hard conversations or threats of "firing" me. I just misread one sentence over text and assumed the worst for too many days leading up to the meeting.

Sometimes we get in our own heads about what God thinks of us, too. But Psalm 119:68 says, "You are good, and what you do is good" (NIV).

God is good by nature! Whenever I echo these words in my head, my faith builds.

Now we're in agreement that God is a good God who loves us and is in control.

Kind of seems like the trifecta, doesn't it?

If we have a good God who loves us and is in control to protect us, that sounds like a God we can trust, right?

But this is the part where our minds beg the question: *If God really is all those things, then why did something bad still happen to me?*

God Makes All Things Work for Our Good

I didn't come up with this on my own. Romans 8:28 tells us this: "And we know that for those who love God all things work together for good, for those who are called according to his purpose" (ESV).

Do you think that if God makes all things work together for good that all those things in their isolated form are "good"?

No!

If everything is inherently good, you don't have to make them come together for the purpose of being good!

But God pulls the bad stuff together and makes it work for good.

When I think of Romans 8:28, I think of the story of Joseph. He was the eleventh son born to a man named Jacob. In total, there were twelve boys in his family.

A testosterone convention, essentially.

Jacob loved his son Joseph more than any of the other brothers, and they all knew it. One day, Joseph went to his brothers to tell them about his dream.

Back in that day, people regarded dreams as symbolic, and they were often prophetic. There was even a person responsible for interpreting dreams in the king's palace. Can you imagine if there were a dream interpreter in corporate businesses? Pretty funny, but very real back in that day.

Joseph told his brothers he had a dream where they all would bow down to him.

Come on, Joseph! You don't say that out loud!

But he did. And his brothers hated him all the more.

One day, Jacob sent Joseph into the fields to find his brothers. When he was on his way over to them, they saw him coming and planned to kill him.

They threw him into a dry well and planned to leave him for dead. While they were eating, they saw a caravan of people coming from afar and headed to Egypt. They got it in their minds to sell Joseph to this group of people rather than kill him.

The Bible tells us in Genesis 37 that Joseph was eventually sold in Egypt to a man named Potiphar, who was one of the king's officials.

You would think being sold into slavery by your own brothers would be hard enough. When Joseph arrived in Egypt, he went through a lot of terrible events, none of which were his fault.

He was wrongly accused of sleeping with his master's wife after she came on to him.

Thrown into prison for years.

Separated from his family.

Wondering what he did to deserve all of this.

If there was a guy who knew about experiencing undeserved consequences, it was Joseph.

But one day, the king needed to have a dream interpreted. One of the palace officials remembered Joseph, currently imprisoned, as a man who interpreted dreams accurately.

The king called for Joseph, and Joseph was able to help protect their land and people from the drought that was to come. Joseph was promoted to second-in-command! Eventually, through an ironic story, he was reunited with his family as well.

Do you think Joseph thought any of that would be the case when he was sitting in a prison cell for twelve years? Absolutely not.

Do you think that as Joseph was sitting in a prison cell, he thought about what his brothers did to him? Probably.

Do you think that Joseph had even a little bitterness toward his brothers? I'd imagine so. I know I would.

God worked those terrible consequences out for Joseph's good to make him second-in-command of a country. Who else do you know who can take slavery, prison, and wrongful accusations and turn it into a prominent position of power with wealth overflowing?

Our God makes all things work together for good. You may be saying, *Okay, I can know that. I can even believe that. But I just can't see how this circumstance is for my good.*

I was right there with you. This brings me to my fifth truth.

God Gives Us Peace

One of the best promises of God is peace beyond what we can understand. Philippians 4:7 says, "And the peace of God, which surpasses all understanding, will guard your hearts and your minds in Christ Jesus" (ESV).

This verse means that when you no longer understand, there can still be peace.

You can know God is good, you can believe that he's in control, you can trust that he loves you, and you can know that he works things together for good.

But the waiting can still be long.

Many of us are in a position where someone hurt us, and it feels like they just got away with it. Perhaps someone took something from us, and we have yet to see God restore it.

> Maybe some of us have had years stolen from us, resources
> taken away, or our reputation impacted. Can I encourage
> you to find peace in the waiting?

I'll never forget hearing the story of John S. Palmer, a pastor in the 1940s through the 1980s. After he graduated from Central Bible Institute in Springfield, Missouri, he moved to Pennsylvania and started a new congregation in the city of New Castle.

He found a one-room elementary school that could serve as a meeting place, and he contacted the school's leaders for permission to hold church services there. Then, he began telling people in the community about the new church, which would meet on Sunday afternoons. All the preparations were coming together, and Palmer was excited to begin this new work.

Two days before the church's opening day, he went to a Friday night meeting at one of his sponsoring churches. Those leaders then passed on a hard message: it had been decided that Palmer would not be the preacher for this new start-up. The job, instead, was being given to one of his friends.

In that moment, they asked him for the keys to the school, and they told Palmer he would be reassigned to another church mission plant. He was never going to attend this place he had worked so hard to organize and had invested his own dollars to build.

Can you imagine the disappointment? Can you imagine the frustration toward God and the church leaders that he must have been feeling?

They had saved their own money. They had cleaned it with their own hands. It was theirs! Yet, it was taken away.

Despite this, John Palmer and his wife, Ruth, went on to pastor several churches throughout their time in ministry. They have seen lives changed by the power of Jesus, and surely God has used them at the other churches they have pastored over the years.

While they didn't understand, they were able to lean on God's peace to move forward and still be used by God.[2]

This brings me to the sixth and final truth.

God Has a Plan

Have you ever been wrestling through a situation and someone hits you with the whole "God's ways are higher than our ways" comment?

The person who said this wasn't wrong, but perhaps it was a poorly timed message as you were grieving. But we know Isaiah tell us, "'My thoughts are nothing like your thoughts,' says the LORD. 'And my ways are far beyond anything you could imagine'" (Isa. 55:8 NLT).

While that might not be the thing we want to hear when we're wrestling through the "why," it's one of the truths I found to give me comfort as I did away with my formula for earning things from God.

The reality is, sometimes God allows us to go through a painful process because he's wanting something from us.

Think of it like the last piece of the puzzle.

He's wanting surrender. You may never get to know why.

At the end of the day, you can know he loves you, he's good, he's in control, he'll work it out, he'll give you peace, and you can still question why.

As I've said throughout this book, questioning why doesn't make you bad; it makes you human. But there must come a point where you say, "I give up. I may never know."

But I know he's good.

> I know he loves me.

> I know he's in control.

> I know he's working it out.

> I know he'll give me peace.

> And I know he has a plan.

That is a God I can surrender my right to understand to.

I'll never forget the last trip we took to visit my grandpa before he passed away. He had severe Alzheimer's but was still living at home with my grandma, who was a doctor. He had gone to bed on the final night, but I remember praying, "God, if there's a way we can have fun with him one more time, I'd really appreciate it."

My grandpa ended up getting out of bed three more times that night and making us laugh. Alzheimer's makes you revert back to when you were younger. A pastor for many years, he came out of his room and started giving my mom and I a sermon—in Italian.

We didn't understand a word, but I recorded it.

After he passed away, I was in New York City for work. I stopped in a pizza parlor in Little Italy and found a guy who could speak Italian. I had him listen to the video.

"It's hard to understand all of it. But the gist of what he's saying is, 'God will take care of it.'"

I couldn't believe it. Here I was in one of the hardest seasons of my life, and years after I recorded that video, God used my grandpa with Alzheimer's to deliver a message I desperately needed.

I don't know the kind of hurt and pain you've been through, and I don't know how God will take care of it, but I need you to know that he will.

For some of us, he's waiting for our surrender. For others, he's hoping we will rest in him in the waiting.

Thirty-nine years after John S. Palmer sought to plant a church in his hometown of New Castle, Pennsylvania, he attended the Ohio District School of Ministry as he was now ministering in Ohio. There, one of the pastors introduced him to his assistant, Curtis Powell, who used to live in New Castle, Pennsylvania.

Powell relayed to him that he had lived with his family on the west side of town. Thirty-eight years ago, he was unsaved and an alcoholic, as was his father. He shared that a young pastor had come to their neighborhood inviting everyone to the new church he was starting at the old schoolhouse.

"Funny thing," he said. "That young pastor never did come back. Another pastor showed up to start the church."

At first, Powell's children attended a Vacation Bible School. Then he began to attend. He was saved and delivered from alcohol. His whole household was saved. He became a helper in the church, and in time, he helped build another church. Thirty-nine years later, Curtis Powell was still serving in the church and walking in freedom.

After thirty-nine years, the Lord allowed John to see and hear a man testifying that he and his family had been saved years ago in that one-room school building on the west side of New Castle. Powell's life was transformed in the church John Palmer had planted but never had the opportunity to lead.

In a message he wrote to his son, John S. Palmer shared these words: "I rejoice because our small and feeble efforts have not been in vain. My disappointment, really, turned out to become God's appointment for my life. For now, two churches have been planted and established . . . the one on the west side of New Castle and the one in Meadville."[3]

How many times do we hope that the mission of the person who hurt us is stifled? Wouldn't it be normal for Palmer to hope that the church that had been taken from him didn't do well?

Can you imagine if he had put all his emotional energy into hoping that the people who wronged him failed in their mission and regretted not making him the pastor?

But he did not have that attitude, and I believe that's why God allowed him to leave a legacy much greater than himself.

While impossible to see in the moment, God was preparing John Palmer for something greater than he could imagine. Not only did the church he prepared flourish and change lives, but the church he went on to pastor changed lives.

Furthermore, Palmer's son went on to pastor a church in Des Moines, Iowa, that, during his tenure, was the largest church in the state. And years after Palmer's son had moved on from pastoring in Iowa, his grandson returned in 2015 and started a church. In a schoolhouse.

You never know what God has in store when you surrender to his plan.

I can't answer why God allowed it. I can't tell you when it will get better. I can't promise you you're going to have your "aha" moment this side of heaven.

But I can promise you that:

the God who's in control,

the God who loves you,

the God who is good,

the God who will work it out,

the God who will give you peace,

that God,

has a plan.

APPLICATION

Write down the truth that you need to remind yourself of the most from this chapter:

Write down some of the truths you've seen evident in your own life about God.

What is one way you're going to remind yourself of these truths?

Prayer: *Lord, you see that I'm struggling with "the why." I pray that you would help me trust. Help me surrender. God, would you continue to show me your sovereignty? Would you remind me how much you love me? And would you give me a peace that passes all understanding? I need you, Lord. Help me to trust in you even when I don't understand. In Jesus's name, amen.*

NOTES

[1] Albert Mehrabian, *Nonverbal Communication* (New Brunswick: Aldine Transaction, 1972), cited in "How Much of Communication Is Nonverbal?," the University of Texas Permian Basin, accessed November 8, 2023, https://online.utpb.edu/about-us/articles/communication/how-much-of-communication-is-nonverbal/.

[2] Story written down by John S. Palmer for his son, John, and related to me through email: John S. Palmer, "How Our Disappointments May Become God's Appointments: A Memoir," email, December 7, 1982.

[3] Palmer, "How Our Disappointments May Become God's Appointments."

"How Do I Know I've FORGIVEN Them?"

What reinforced my desire to write this book was a conversation with my husband when he blatantly told me that I had not forgiven the people who had hurt me. I had even prefaced my thoughts to him with, "I've forgiven them, but . . ."

While I knew he was right, the hardest time I had with him saying that is it went against all of the work I had put in to try to forgive. I had been trying, and trying, and trying. It just wasn't over yet.

My mom has always told me feelings don't know time.

The basis for that comment is that, over time, we think things should get better. Perhaps we even do make significant progress toward healing with God's help and the gift of time.

And then their picture pops up on your feed. Then you run into them at the store. Maybe you know of a time when you're going to run into them and you're dreading it.

If you see each encounter with them as a test to determine if you've healed, you may fail every time. Feelings don't know time.

In the book *The Body Keeps the Score* by Bessel van der Kolk, he talks about how trauma is stored in an area of the brain that we can't even really access. This part of the brain is responsible for hormones and adrenals, but it is not something that our thoughts can necessarily control.

If you have experienced what you believe to be significant trauma, I would recommend seeking professional help through therapy. There is no shame in doing so.

But regardless of whether most people would call what we've experienced as traumatic, this study speaks to the fact that we need healing beyond just thinking positively.

You may be able to mask unforgiveness and bitterness for a time. Then, when you see the person or experience one of your triggers, you wonder why it doesn't feel like you've made any progress. Give yourself some grace.

Just because your heart starts racing and your brain can't focus doesn't mean you haven't made progress.

I remember a season in my life when the hurt I experienced was occupying so many more thoughts than just times when I was triggered. It felt like an every-minute, every-hour kind of thing.

The process of forgiveness is the only way to fully combat this.

Many of us are familiar with stages of grief. I believe there are also stages to forgiveness. I would define total forgiveness as an active pardoning of an offender or wrongdoer, whether they deserve it or not, and a release of bitterness, resentment, and vengeance toward them.

Psychologists will tell you that the stages of grief can occur in any order, and you may jump back to stages at any given point. With these stages of forgiveness, I believe God is calling us to see each stage as a step that we are progressing forward on. If we need to repeat a step or go back, there isn't shame, but, unlike the stages of grief, we are actively working to move on to the next step in forgiveness.

The Steps of Forgiveness

1. Recognition
2. Remembrance
3. Release
4. Rest

1. Recognition

As we discussed in the first chapter, the first thing we need to do is recognize our hurt. All the experts in the world cannot cure an unnamed, misunderstood disease. Similarly, we need to recognize what hurt us most.

I like how C. S. Lewis reminds us that "forgiveness is not excusing."[1]

We are not minimizing what they did or the pain they caused. Many of us get stuck in unforgiveness simply because we have a hard time naming the offense. This may be because of guilt, shame, excusing, denial, or a tendency to set aside our own feelings. Regardless of the reason, your first order of business is to recognize the hurt and name the offense.

2. Remembrance

Second, as Christians, we need to remember what Jesus did for us on the cross. When we remember what Jesus did for us, we are reminded that Jesus forgave a debt that we could never repay.

As we humble ourselves, we are reminded that we, too, need forgiveness and therefore we can forgive one another. Just like in the parable of the servant who was forgiven of a debt he could never repay, let us not be the one to turn around and be unwilling to forgive lesser debts.

As we've been going through this journey, I recognize there may be one question in the back of your mind that you're afraid to bring up: *What if I'm in the wrong, too?*

We have talked about forgiving with the assumption that we are not at fault, but we know that in most circumstances, both parties have something to do with it.

Even if they are able to admit that they had something to do with it, many people will make themselves feel better by saying, *But they were more in the wrong!*

That may be the case. I felt that way in my circumstances. But it didn't change the fact that the other person experienced pain because of me.

The Bible gives guidance for when we're fully or partially in the wrong. We should go to the person, confess our sins or apologize for any offense, and ask for forgiveness.

Whether intentional or not, I had a hard time with the fact that I hurt someone.

In my situation, I remember being so upset. I was not aware that my actions had hurt them, but when they brought it to my attention, I was very sad. I cried several times and begged for forgiveness. I went to them and shared from deep within my soul in an effort to explain why I did what I did or said what I said.

After months of trying to convince the person that I was genuinely sorry, I was still discouraged that I hadn't received their forgiveness. I remember punishing myself as a way to prove to them that I really was sorry.

One day, I was driving to church, and I remember praying, "God, please! Please forgive me! Please help them to forgive me!"

God answered back so clearly it was almost audible to me:

Lauren, they may never forgive you. But I have forgiven you. And now it's time that you forgive yourself.

That moment changed my life.

Should we try not to hurt people in the first place? Absolutely.

Are there action steps we can take to show the person that our apology is genuine and that we care about them? Definitely.

But there comes a point where their forgiveness journey is theirs, and you do not need to continue to punish yourself to try to win their forgiveness or acceptance.

It was from that encounter with God that I realized what not forgiving myself was doing.

A. Breaking Free from Bondage

I realized that, in an attempt to prove to them I was really sorry, I was inflicting pain upon myself.

I would try to be notably sad around them, I was heaping guilt and shame upon myself, and I was living with the regret of my actions.

I had embraced so much shame for unintentionally hurting someone that I stopped getting together with other friends both as a way to punish myself and out of fear that I may hurt them.

The problem with this was, no matter what actions I took, I didn't earn their forgiveness.

I tried so hard to punish myself for them to accept my apology, and believe me, it didn't make the situation any better.

Eventually, I felt God was calling for me to be free as the offender, just as he has called each victim to break free of the bondage of unforgiveness through forgiveness.

B. Realizing That We Are Not Higher Than God

What does it say to our sovereign God that his forgiveness of us is not enough?

When God told me that he had forgiven me, that should have been enough. But I was saying, *You may accept and forgive me, God, but I'm really waiting for my own acceptance and forgiveness.*

I was putting myself ahead of God. I wasn't satisfied until either the person I offended forgave me or until I decided to forgive myself. I didn't really care that the God of this universe would forgive me.

That was a huge mistake! The God of this universe sent his only Son to die for us so that we may have life! He is the ultimate judge. What he says goes.

We should absolutely accept that because God forgives us, we are able to live in freedom!

To wait on anything more is to place someone ahead of God.

As you remember what Christ did for you on the cross, I pray you are able to both forgive them and forgive yourself. For it is only by remembering what Christ did that we can fully release.

3. Release

First, we must name the offense, and after remembering what Christ did for us, we are able to release the hurt. That's the work we've been doing throughout this whole book. There are many reasons to hold on to bitterness with a tight grip. However, there is freedom, joy, restoration, and peace that comes with releasing.

I want to address a question that often comes up when discussing forgiveness. The question is: *What if they don't apologize?*

The answer is no different than if they do apologize. An apology does not automatically mean we have forgiven in our heart. Rather, we still need to do the work of forgiveness. God calls us to release people from things they don't even realize they did to us! Forgiveness is for our benefit.

Of course, it is harder to forgive someone when there isn't recognition or understanding that they hurt you. It would be easy to say that they are undeserving of forgiveness. But aren't we all undeserving of forgiveness?

At the beginning of this book, we said we would follow Paul's advice and "take every thought captive" (2 Cor. 10:5 ESV) to wage war against bitterness. While I do not want to minimize the injustice felt when your offender shows no remorse, we need to be careful that it is not used as an excuse to hold on to unforgiveness.

In Miroslav Volf's book *Free of Charge*, he writes, "Forgiving the unrepentant is not an optional extra in the Christian way of life; it's the heart of the thing."[2]

Please, friend, do not be held captive to an apology. Release them from their offense so you can move on to rest.

4. Rest

Ultimately, you can know you've forgiven when you can wish them well. One of the greatest tests for beating bitterness is if you can pray for the one who hurt you. No, not a prayer that their car breaks down or that they are miserable. The Bible says, "Love your enemies and pray for those who persecute you" (Matt. 5:44 NIV). The human side of me shudders a little even writing that. I know how hard this can be. Yet, when you can wish someone well despite the pain they've caused you, you have finally forgiven to completion. Before you can complete the steps, I want to address two common questions to bring closure to the process.

Do I have to restore my relationship with the other person?

No.

Sometimes we think that we must prove to ourselves that we've forgiven by being friends with them again or even by trusting them again in a romantic relationship, but that wisdom is misguided.

Did David go to Saul and say, "Hey Saul, I know you've tried to kill me multiple times, but I just want to make sure that we're good, right?" No.

Sometimes, restoration of the relationship is not needed or wise.

It's easy to think that for things to be completely restored you need to be in relationship with that person again, but that's not what the Bible tells us.

You are welcome to set boundaries for your life that allow you to move forward without embracing the relationship again.

One element that's hard about this is people around you may see it as something that needs to happen for them to feel like you've forgiven. But that is not the case, either.

Some also wonder if they need to address their feelings with the other person as a way to reconcile.

When I say reconcile, what I mean is to coexist or be on good terms with one another, even if you are not in close relations with them. Reconciliation is beautiful, healing, and can be very beneficial for people. But it is not always the best course.

In my situation, I strongly felt that to address it would not lead to healing but rather more pain and could lead to further misunderstandings.

I chose not to reconcile with the other person, but that doesn't mean I shouldn't strive to be at peace with them in my own heart. Our goal should always be to live peaceably with one another for reasons we've already discussed.

The last question that plagues people who long to forgive but don't feel they have yet is: *Did I really forgive if I keep having to?*

Yes, you likely really forgave even if those thoughts and emotions keep coming up.

The Bible tells us forgiveness is a cycle.

When Peter asked Jesus how often he should forgive someone, he thought seven times would put him in the clear. Jesus corrected him and said seventy times seven (Matt. 18:21–22)!

Okay, where are my people who are good at math? Seventy times seven is four hundred ninety.

$70 \times 7 = 490$

But Jesus wasn't talking about starting a tally and no longer forgiving once you've hit your max number. He wasn't even referencing a large number to say that you must forgive beyond what you can count.

The number seven has biblical significance. Traditionally, the number seven meant "fullness" or "completeness."[3]

This is confirmed in multiple ways in Genesis 1. First, the Bible says that on the seventh day of creation, God rested (Gen. 2:2).

This is symbolic because we see how, after seven days, the creation of earth was complete, and it gave way to rest. It's important to note that the creation story is not fully complete without that seventh day of rest.

Furthermore, each of the key words in Genesis 1:1 is repeated by multiples of seven in Genesis 1:2–2:3.

"God" = 35 times (7 x 5)

"Land" = 21 times (7 x 3)

"Skies" = 21 times (7 x 3)

"Light" = 7 times

"Day" = 7 times[4]

God continues to use the number seven to symbolize completion, fulfillment, and rest throughout the Bible. For example, we see the number seven used symbolically throughout the book of Revelation as well.

When Jesus said seventy times seven, he was not just talking about 490. He was saying, *Forgive until completion. Forgive until fulfillment.* Forgive until you have rest.

That in its very nature would suggest that there is a cycle to forgiveness that we must continue doing until it's complete.

I find great comfort in this quote by C. S. Lewis: "There is no use of talking as if forgiveness is easy. For we find that the work of forgiveness has to be done over and over again."[5]

Forgiveness is a cycle.

It is not a thought cycle like the one I discussed at the start that was full of bitterness and hurt. Rather, forgiveness is a cycle until we complete it.

That's what I hope this book has done for you. Next time you have one of the thoughts referenced in each chapter, my hope is that this book has given you the tools to answer each one in a biblical way that leads you back to forgiveness. You're then able to do this until completion.

Practical Ways to Practice Forgiveness

My goal is that by now you have committed to the act of forgiveness, but here are some practical tips to help you live it out:

1. Take Ownership of Your Thoughts

We need more than just positive thoughts to heal, but we certainly need to learn to control our thought life if we are going to move forward for good.

I'm amazed at the number of people who want to find freedom, but most evenings they're on social media looking up the people who've wronged them to see if they're as miserable as they hope.

Spoiler alert: no one looks miserable on social media. Even if they did, you're not doing yourself any favors by devoting thoughts to them.

Caroline Leaf, author of *Switch On Your Brain*, says this: "When you think, you build thoughts, and these become physical substances in your brain."[6]

That's why the premise of this book is based in thoughts that we keep repeating to ourselves over and over that leave us stuck in the past.

Sometimes we think our thoughts aren't impacting our future, but, my friend, that couldn't be further from the truth.

God is desiring that we move on! And it starts with our thought life.

2. Stop Talking about It
This is the concept God taught me that stopped me in my tracks.

My sister used to joke that every coffee date I had with a friend would be three hours or it didn't count. I have nothing against a good coffee date, but I want to encourage you to watch your conversations as well as your thoughts.

You can't expect to be talking about the past and simultaneously be moving forward into the present.

I think about the Israelites when they left Egypt. The Israelites were up against the Red Sea with the Egyptians in hot pursuit of them. The Israelites started complaining because they couldn't see God's plan. They kept looking to the past and even suggested that life was better in Egypt—when they were enslaved!

Finally, in Exodus 14:15, the Lord responded: "Why are you crying out to me? Tell the Israelites to move on" (NIV).

It wasn't that God didn't understand their fear. It wasn't that he didn't think their desire for safety was valid.

It was that God wanted to do a new thing!

Move on!

The English Standard Version says, "Go forward." The Common English Bible says, "Get moving."

God has more for you up ahead. If you do not move forward, you will be like the Israelites: a sitting duck.

Whatever they took from you, don't let them take another minute, another thought, or another conversation.

3. Replace the Old with the New

I remember reading books that told me to get ahold of my life and move on.

Okay! I thought. *I'm going to do that!*

There was just one problem. I had already built thought patterns. To Leaf's point earlier, these thoughts had already turned into physical substances. They were habits. I could see the value in no longer thinking and talking about things, but I couldn't just flip a switch and make it so.

That's when I remembered the Bible tells you what to think about (Phil. 4:8). It tells us to think about things that are lovely or praiseworthy. Things that are pure and right. The sun in the sky, the beauty of the season, the five things you're grateful for that day. Think about the good things!

This verse isn't a command as much as it is great life advice! It serves as a guide for what we should think about.

We need to recognize that when we stop thinking about something, it gives way to a whole lot of empty space that Satan wants to continue to fill with the wrong thought patterns.

We need to begin thinking about the noble, the right, the pure, the lovely, and the praiseworthy.

Examples of this could be thinking about things you're grateful for. If you're having a bad day, think about a great vacation you have coming up or a fun one you had in the past. Dwell on the "things above," as Colossians 3:2 (NIV) says.

Another trick for thinking about great things is looking outside. Even if the weather is bad, there is usually beauty somewhere around! I live in Iowa—if I can find good from looking outside in any season, you can too!

It's important to replace the memories with thoughts that are excellent or praiseworthy.

I remember my counselor telling me a story about a lady whose husband had died from a car crash in a snowstorm. He was only out driving to get ingredients for his wife to bake a cake.

On the scene of the accident, there were ingredients like flour and sugar all over the car.

The lady proclaimed that she was never baking a cake again. Her counselor encouraged her to do the opposite.

"Bake the cake," she said. "You need to make new memories to heal from the old ones."

That last comment has stuck with me to this day. Too often, we avoid going to that restaurant or that place or even that city because it reminds us of a painful memory.

There's something beautiful about being able to create new memories in a space that we can draw on whenever we are trying to move on.

Don't just avoid the thoughts or memories—replace them with new ones! Bake the cake.

Okay, Did It Work?

When you picked up this book, you were probably looking for your solution to forgiveness.

A way to stop thinking about it. A way to stop hurting from it. A way to stop having fake conversations with your adversary in the shower.

I can't promise you that you won't be tempted to do these things. I still am.

But my prayer for you is that through this process we've:

1. Exposed the lie of bitterness in our lives
2. Recognized the freedom in forgiveness
3. Gained the tools to combat toxic (but normal) thoughts so we can move forward to our best years

APPLICATION

When I feel stuck in the unforgiveness cycle . . .

I'm going to remind myself . . .

I'm going to decide to . . .

Instead of dwelling on it, I'm going to choose to think about . . .

My prayer for you: *God, I pray for the wonderful son or daughter who's reading this book. I pray that your presence would come upon them. I pray that they would continue to see the lie of bitterness and unforgiveness in any instance in their lives. Give them the tools and the strength to forgive. Open their eyes to the freedom of forgiveness. I pray that their best years would be ahead of them. I pray that the latter would be greater than the former and that you would ignite your people to walk in freedom to fulfill the mission you've placed on each of our lives. In Jesus's name, amen!*

I love you all.

NOTES

[1] Lewis, *The Weight of Glory*, 178.

[2] Miroslav Volf, *Free of Charge: Giving and Forgiving in a Culture Stripped of Grace* (Grand Rapids: Zondervan, 2005), 209.

[3] Maurice H. Farbridge, *Studies in Biblical and Semitic Symbolism* (Eugene, OR: Wipf and Stock, 2007), 134–37.

[4] Tim Mackie and Jon Collins, "The Significance of Seven," *BibleProject* (podcast), October 21, 2019, https://bibleproject.com/podcast/significance-7/.

[5] C. S. Lewis, *Reflections on the Psalms* (1961; reis., San Francisco: HarperOne, 2017), 28.

[6] Caroline Leaf, *Switch on Your Brain: The Key to Peak Happiness, Thinking, and Health* (Ada, MI: Baker Books, 2015), 25.

Stay connected to Lauren!

 youtube.com/@laurnvanderlinden

 @lauren.vanderlinden

 laurenvanderlinden.com

And you can find more resources here:

laurenvanderlinen.com/resources

WHEN IT HURTS TO HOPE

RACHEL MILLER

Embrace the tension of unmet longing and choose hope—even when life doesn't look like you thought it would.

ISBN 978-1-68426-298-4

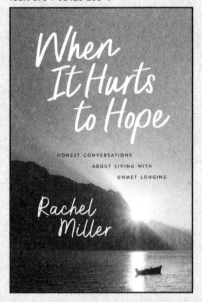

Maybe you've chosen to bury your dreams, denying your desires and sleepwalking through life. Maybe you've let your longing take the driver's seat and now you feel frantic and out of control. Even worse, you find yourself growing cold to God, wondering, *If I never get what I want, is God still good?* This book tackles that hard question—and many others.

When It Hurts to Hope will show you the middle ground between burying your longings and overindulging them. Rachel Miller offers encouragement and practical advice on how to honor God and honor your desires at the same time, sharing tools for being emotionally and spiritually healthy. Through storytelling, Scripture, and humor, this book will help you choose hope in tough seasons like unwanted singleness, infertility, chronic illness, and career frustrations. Ultimately, Jesus is the only one who can meet every longing.

1-877-816-4455 toll free
www.leafwoodpublishers.com

LEAFWOOD
PUBLISHERS
an imprint of Abilene Christian University Press